"I grew up in church and wc [...] and people would say stuff like, 'This is worth dying for.' But I didn't feel that way. I felt like something was missing. Fast-forward decades later, and I was reading Andrew Farley's book on a flight to Australia. By the time we landed, I was blown away. It made me think, 'If this is who Christ really is, then yes, *this* is worth dying for!' *Relaxing with God* is Andrew's latest work, and it could change everything for you. Expect to discover the freedom of God's grace. Expect to know Jesus like never before!"

—**Bart Millard,** lead singer for MercyMe

"Andrew Farley is clearheaded and straight-shooting on argu-ably the most important topic ever: grace. He is, thankfully, a dog on a bone when it comes to the grace of God and won't let his readers wiggle away from the beauty and majesty of God's grace toward them. Because of his clarity and consistency, Andrew is powerfully used by God to switch on the light for many people. I'm grateful to have encountered his writing, and I'm always excited when I meet another reader who has experienced the Farley Factor."

—**Bruxy Cavey,** teaching pastor at The Meeting House, bestselling author of *The End of Religion*

"Andrew Farley is one of those bright, bright lights in this generation, calling us back to the original Good News. The way he communicates about God's grace helps convince us that these truths are not just theology to compare but life to free us. I'm very proud to stand alongside this man."

—**John Lynch,** bestselling coauthor of *Bo's Cafe* and *The Cure*, team member at TrueFaced

"Among all of today's Christian pastors, teachers, and authors, there is only one whose work I never miss: Andrew Farley. He offers the most consistently invigorating, surprisingly relevant, Bible-based messages of anyone I know. If you want truth that blows away the cobwebs in your heard and speaks directly to your heart, *Relaxing with God* is your book."

—**Ralph Harris,** president of LifeCourse Ministries,
author of *God's Astounding Opinion of You*

"Very few Christians know what it means to rest in Christ. But as Andrew writes, rest is Jesus's promise to every believer. Are you ready to loosen your grip on all the religious traditions? Are you ready to let go of all the worry and self-effort? If so, I encourage you to read this book carefully. Soak in the truth of God's love and grace. It's time for you to relax with God and enjoy his life to the full."

—**Bob Christopher,** president of Basic Gospel
(BasicGospel.net)

"There's nothing better than kicking back and just loving life. Belly-laughing, crying because you can, and cherishing unfiltered relationship with someone you trust are rare treasures in our overstimulated society. It's time to relax and experience God: his smile, his serenity, and his extravagant love and acceptance. *Relaxing with God* is an engaging book for anyone who dares to accept the invitation. Your life will never be the same!"

—**Audrey Meisner,** bestselling author of *Marriage Under Cover*; TV host of *My New Day*

"Andrew Farley's message beckons the believer away from treadmill tactics and self-righteous religiosity. He consistently invites the church to a place of rest won by love and offered by grace. His message has helped people in our church find freedom from unbiblical thinking and courage to experience the life we are meant to live."

—**Steve Benedict,** pastor of Grace Life Community Church,
Bristow, Virginia

"Andrew Farley is one of the best communicators of our day. *Relaxing with God* was written for those who want to walk with God and reflect his heart to a hurting world. I wholeheart-edly recommend this book. It will make you wonder how on earth you could have missed these simple, powerful truths of the gospel!"

"I keep falling deeper in love with Jesus as a result of Andrew Farley's ability to communicate the simplicity of God's grace with such precision. *Relaxing with God* is yet another triumph in making the main thing the main thing. This book shows us all how to experience true freedom in Jesus Christ. And in him, we can finally relax!"

"We've been touched by the depth and clarity of Andrew Far-ley's revelations concerning the believer's total forgiveness and union with Christ. What freedom to live *from* God rather than merely living for him. Read this book and begin relaxing with God!"

"Andrew Farley's writing never ceases to amaze me. As a pas-tor myself, I believe that the gospel of grace is the only hope for mankind, and nobody I've ever read articulates it more clearly than Andrew. I recommend every book he's written, and I can't recommend *Relaxing with God* highly enough. If your relationship with Christ seems to have been downgraded to little more than the stress of religious obligation, it's time to recapture your joy! Read this great book, and I'm confident you'll discover what you've been missing."

RELAXING
WITH
GOD

THE NEGLECTED SPIRITUAL DISCIPLINE

ANDREW FARLEY

BakerBooks
a division of Baker Publishing Group
Grand Rapids, Michigan

Published by Baker Books
a division of Baker Publishing Group
P.O. Box 6287, Grand Rapids, MI 49516-6287
www.bakerbooks.com

Printed in the United States of America

Library of Congress Cataloging-in-Publication Data is on file at the Library of Congress, Washington, DC.

ISBN 978-0-8010-1518-2

Unless otherwise indicated, Scripture quotations are from the Holy Bible, New International Version®. NIV®. Copyright © 1973, 1978, 1984, 2011 by Biblica, Inc.™ Used by permission of Zondervan. All rights reserved worldwide. www.zondervan.com

Scripture quotations labeled Message are from *The Message* by Eugene H. Peterson, copyright © 1993, 1994, 1995, 2000, 2001, 2002. Used by permission of NavPress Publishing Group. All rights reserved.

Scripture quotations labeled NASB are from the New American Standard Bible®, copyright © 1960, 1962, 1963, 1968, 1971, 1972, 1973, 1975, 1977, 1995 by The Lockman Foundation. Used by permission.

Scripture quotations labeled NIV 1984 are from the Holy Bible, New International Version®. NIV®. Copyright © 1973, 1978, 1984 by Biblica, Inc.™ Used by permission of Zondervan. All rights reserved worldwide. www.zondervan.com

Scripture quotations labeled NKJV are from the New King James Version. Copyright © 1982 by Thomas Nelson, Inc. Used by permission. All rights reserved.

Italics in Scripture are the author's emphasis.

Published in association with the literary agency of Alive Communications, Inc., 7680 Goddard Street, Suite 200, Colorado Springs, CO 80920, alivecommunications.com.

14   15   16   17   18   19   20   7   6   5   4   3   2   1

Contents

INTRODUCTION

1

My Victoria Secret

I definitely would have gone to jail. You don't just stand up in an auditorium and stop a *Saturday Night Live* star during their comedy routine and get away with it. And especially not with what I planned to say!

I had received a message from God. My task was to interrupt Victoria Jackson's routine and preach the gospel to more than one thousand Furman University students that Friday evening. At the end, I was to lead them in the sinner's prayer.

I sat in my apartment, only a few miles away, agonizing over the call to action. This was the latest in a series of demands that I felt God had placed on me.

Until then, I had complied with every one.

Camp Sin

It all started with my Christian education. I went to chapel every week for thirteen years. And every week throughout high school, we heard the same thing. Even if the sermon did seem new and fresh at first, it would somehow meander back to the same place.

About two-thirds of the way through, the speaker would tell us we needed to recommit to God, work harder, and do more than we'd been doing. Sometimes this would mean coming forward in front of the whole school and "taking a stand." Other times it would involve some kneeling.

If we were away on a school retreat, they'd offer a ceremonial campfire. Some of us would confess our sins out loud, then write them down, throw the paper into the fire, and watch it burn. No matter what form this purging took, it was sure to include public embarrassment for some, maybe even some wailing for others.

Some would confess their love for rock music, while others would admit they hadn't been doing their quiet times lately. Still others would own up to their lack of boldness when they had an opportunity to share Christ and dropped the ball.

The speakers always seemed pleased to stir up these admissions. I guess they felt they'd been used by God to pull out our sins publicly. You know, into the light.

"This was so great for the kids! We'll definitely have to invite the speaker back next year," we'd hear the teachers whisper.

Pant Legs

Year after year, these events were perpetuating an emotional cycle: commit, try hard, fail, feel horrible, then confess and recommit to try even harder, only to have your hopes of renewal shattered all over again. It seemed so spiritual, but it set me up for what was to come.

I never took Christianity too seriously in high school, as it appeared to mean sacrificing a lot of fun. At our school, being a good Christian meant your hair was cut above your ears and your pant legs weren't rolled up. In the 1980s, rolling up your pant legs was what the world did. And good Christians didn't want to be of this world.

But physical appearance was only the beginning. There was rule upon rule, and I was left with the impression that you either go all out with this Christianity thing or you just barely squeak by. There was really no sense in landing somewhere in the middle. Therefore, I ignored most of the behavior improvement program. I wanted to enjoy myself in high school, so I stuffed down the shame.

The Addiction

When I started college, I decided that I was tired of feeling like the black sheep in God's family. It was high time that I take my faith seriously. Given what I'd heard, that basically meant two things: Bible study and witnessing. So I began doing those things, and doing them more than anyone else I had ever met.

I started by teaching Bible studies in the campus ministries. Then I progressed to volunteering at the local halfway house, where I witnessed to ex-prisoners and taught them the way to salvation. Then I went off to Greece and Italy to study for a semester. It was there that I began street witnessing. I'd skip my classes to have more time on the streets to confront people and save their souls. My grades suffered, yes, but in the name of Jesus.

In Europe, the addiction really took root. And upon my return to the United States, things intensified. I shared Christ in jail cells, on airplanes, and even during my university classes. I'd proselytize during gym class as we were working out. And in speech class I'd make presentations, for a grade, on how to get saved.

I got a C on the first speech, and things went south from there. We were assigned to give a variety of speeches throughout the semester—for example, a persuasive speech and a procedural how-to speech. So I tried to *persuade* my classmates to get saved, and then later that semester I showed them the *procedure* for how to get saved. They were going to hear the same thing, over and over again, until they got it.

Whether they liked it or not.

Door-to-Door

On trips home to Virginia, I began witnessing, door-to-door, in my parents' neighborhood. My parents would go to work each day, and then so would I. After all, I was driven. I believed I was going about the Lord's work. So I wouldn't stop. Or I couldn't stop. Or maybe it was both.

Yes, some people were making decisions to believe in Jesus. Whether they truly understood what they were deciding, I'm not sure to this day. And whether God really used any of that, I can't say. But I do know this—as I look back, I can easily see that it was all for me. It was all about me feeling whole again. It was all about me finding relief from my guilt and shame and doing whatever I needed to do to please God and to get him to like me again. At least until the next hoop I needed to jump through came along.

And the next challenge was always just a bit more grandiose.

The Town and Country

"Son, get in the car and drive away as fast as you can! The restaurant owner called the cops, and they're coming for you," my dad said to me with more concern than I had ever seen on his face.

We'd been eating breakfast together in the Town and Country restaurant in New Baltimore, Virginia. It wasn't that often that I got to enjoy a nice breakfast with my dad, at least not since I had moved away for college. But I ruined breakfast with him that morning, because I stood up and started to preach. Yeah, to the whole restaurant. When I got to the invitation part, some lady said she'd be interested in receiving Christ. So I sat down in her booth and prayed with her while the manager was calling the cops.

Strangely, something good may have come from it. But I was definitely disturbing the peace. And the restaurant owner was *not* happy about it.

The police station wasn't too far away, so I didn't have much time. My dad got up to talk with the owner to try to smooth things over. I bolted out the door and escaped to serve God another day.

Comfort Inn

While at home in Virginia, I began working at a Comfort Inn in Chantilly. My job was to mow the lawn, clean the pool, and help with general maintenance. The problem was that although I needed the money, my only real agenda seemed to be saving people.

An airline company was holding a flight attendant training seminar in the hotel conference room. Now, I had shared the gospel numerous times with *individuals* at the hotel, one-on-one. But this was my chance to reach a lot of people, all at once. So I charged into the room without hesitation. I interrupted the speaker midsentence and began shouting the gospel to the roomful of flight attendants.

I was able to utter about fifteen sentences—you know, the essentials—without taking a breath. Then I led them in a prayer of salvation. When I said "Amen" and opened my eyes, the seminar leader said I should come back later if I had more to say. He announced that anyone who wanted to hear more could stay during their lunch break.

When I returned at the break, one lady was waiting for me. She said she was already a Christian, but she admired my boldness. She said she wished she could be like me.

If only she knew.

That was my last day working at the Comfort Inn. Yeah, they fired me. I guess I wasn't *that* good at cleaning the pool.

The Vienna Metro

The Vienna station was at the end of the subway line that stretched farthest south into Virginia. I'd drive up to the

Park and Ride, buy my ticket, and jump on the train. I knew I'd have a captive audience there.

I'd pick a subway car and ride along to the next station. This gave me a few minutes to yell the gospel at the top of my lungs to the entire train car. I knew my lines really well. I'd tell them they were sinners. I'd tell them Christ died for them. Then I'd tell them he offered new life. I'd even have an altar call of sorts, right there on the train.

I got very little response, but that didn't stop me. I'd hop off at the next stop, pick a new car, and start all over.

Now that's commitment, right? Well, I guess. Maybe those chapel speakers from high school would be proud. Wouldn't they? But why was I so *miserable* inside?

Freezer Aisle

Evangelism had become a drug. I felt great when I'd just shared Christ with someone. And I couldn't wait until the next opportunity.

Literally, I *couldn't* wait.

I'd seek a new high the minute my buzz began fading. I assumed that was the Holy Spirit commanding me to keep moving, to "be radical."

If I went to bed without sharing Christ with someone that day, I couldn't sleep. I'd haul myself out of bed, drive to the nearest twenty-four-hour grocery store, and share Christ with someone in the freezer aisle. But most shoppers were more concerned about escaping from me *and* the coldest section of the store. It didn't work, but it gave me that warm feeling inside so I could sleep one more night in peace.

That was all that really mattered.

My Victoria Secret

But I had a secret, one that I was very ashamed of at the time. And I hadn't told anyone. I bailed on the God of the universe when he'd sent me on my most important mission yet.

In my mind, God was calling me to interrupt Victoria Jackson's standup comedy routine on a Friday night at Furman University's McAlister Auditorium. I was to climb up onstage in front of my peers, brush little Victoria off to the side, and begin my invitation. This would be the largest audience I had impacted for Jesus!

I didn't even drive over there. I chickened out. And I lay on the floor of my apartment curled up in the fetal position, bawling my eyes out. I had let God down this time, and I knew I'd have to pay. This was the beginning of my crash into a state of religious anxiety and depression that would last for several years.

Relaxing with God

I was doing everything that anyone had ever suggested in order to grow spiritually and feel closer to God. I was praying all the time. I was studying my Bible for hours a day. And believe me, I was sharing my faith!

My belief system was both complicated and exhausting. And it wasn't working. Despite my sincere commitment to

God, I had nothing to show for it. No peace. No joy. No nothing. I was going to heaven, but there was nothing about my present life that appealed to anyone, that's for sure.

That was twenty-three years ago.

Now *everything* has changed. Today, I know exactly how to soak in the unconditional grace of God, to allow his Spirit to flood my mind with thoughts of his love and acceptance. I know how to enjoy my safety and security in Jesus and how to allow God to transmit his radiant life through mine. I no longer battle guilt and fear, and the path ahead is not foggy. Now I celebrate Jesus like never before, and I'd wish my life on anyone.

How did everything change? Did I just ease off or completely stop all spiritual activity? No, today I probably do more talking about Jesus than ever. But things are different on the *inside*. Through my experience of crashing and burning and having to start all over again, God taught me some truths that literally saved my life. He taught me *how* to relax. He taught me that he *wanted* me to relax. And he taught me to *live from rest* in a way that I had never known.

And what God taught me is in this book.

2

The Opposite of Every Sermon You've Ever Heard?

You may not have gone to the extremes that I did, but many of us fall victim to the desire to get ourselves in shape for God. Genuine as that desire may be, it only creates unrest as we're bound up by an intricate web of rules or tied down by a nebulous sense that we're not meeting God's demands.

Meanwhile, Jesus told us his yoke is *easy*. He said his burden is *light*. He claimed we'd find *rest* for our souls (Matt. 11:29–30).

We know that's got to be real, somehow.

Still, how can we relax when we keep heaping on more and more performance demands that only fuel *un*rest? Take a minute to ponder how many "challenges" you've heard in your lifetime as a Christian. How many times have you been asked to step out of your comfort zone, to give until it hurts, and to "be radical" for God? On top of these commitments, you've been presented with three steps to financial freedom and four keys to a successful marriage. Maybe you've been told there are five types of prayer and seven spiritual disciplines. At the local bookstore, you find Bible-based diet and fasting guides and Christian exercise programs (look out for my upcoming release of *Pontius Pilates: Getting Fit the Roman Way!*). Apparently, you can't even make dinner or work on your abs without getting a preacher involved!

Slowly and subtly, we might get the impression that Christianity is largely about *performing*. We start to think that we need formulas or long lists of instructions to be "good" Christians—to get right and stay right with God.

That's exhausting!

Restless Rhetoric

Sure, we Christians might feel great knowing we're on our way to heaven. But in the back of our minds, many of us are still plagued by what we imagine we're supposed to be doing for God and how much we're *not* actually doing for him. We've been subtly fed a long "to-do for God" list, and within today's flavors of Christian teaching, it seems the default setting is complicated, not simple. Have you ever stopped to consider the convoluted, hollow ideas we've ended up with?

Here are some examples:

- We're not under the Old Testament law, but we should still use it as a "compass" to lead us.

21

- We can give freely from the heart, not under any pressure, but it better be at least 10 percent.
- We can't "be perfect" like Jesus taught, but we should still strive to meet the standard we can't meet.
- Our old sinner self died with Christ, but we're still sinners who need to die to self.
- We've been forgiven and cleansed by Jesus's blood, but we need to ask God to forgive and cleanse us every day.
- The punishment for our sins fell on Christ, but God will judge us for our sins.
- We're already right with God through Jesus's sacrifice, but we examine ourselves at communion to "get right with God."
- God chose us for salvation, but it may feel like we chose God, and we just can't understand this until heaven.

Do you see what I see? Is *this* the truth that sets us free? No, it's just a bunch of double-talk! Am I forgiven or not? Am I free or not? Am I a new creation or not? Am I close to God or not? Without definitive answers to these questions, we will never find ourselves relaxing with God. And we can't know what it means to *live* from rest on a daily basis.

God's way is much simpler: "And now I'm afraid that exactly as the Snake seduced Eve with his smooth patter, *you are being lured away from the simple purity of your love for Christ*" (2 Cor. 11:3 Message). So what if things don't need to be complicated and confusing? What if it's all supposed to be so simple that even a child can get it?

As we wrestle with the idea of relaxing with God, our current "programming"—the way we've always believed or done things—may attempt to steal our newfound freedom.

So I ask you to keep a couple of questions in mind as you read this book. Here they are:

- Do I genuinely believe that God's message through Jesus is supposed to be *simple*?
- Do I genuinely believe that the gospel is designed to bring me to a place of real, spiritual *relaxation*?

The Opposite of Every Sermon You've Ever Heard?

Of course, there are lots of great sermons out there. But a quick internet search of sermon archives worldwide reveals hardly any sermons on relaxing with God and very few on the topic of spiritual rest in general. I guess it just doesn't seem right to us to even think about relaxing when it comes to our Christian faith.

But what if I told you there's an incredible paradox to discover here? It's that work comes from rest, that the kind of works that please God actually come from our relaxing with him. This is why the author of Hebrews tells us to "make every effort to enter that rest" (4:11).

Make every *effort* to rest? Yes, apparently it takes a concerted effort on our part to get to the place where we can truly relax with God.

Still not sure that rest should be our focus? Take a minute to consider the fruit of the Spirit—things like love, peace, kindness, gentleness, and patience (Gal. 5:22–23). Do we really think these can come from a place of spiritual effort as we try our best to crank them out? No, these attributes are birthed from an attitude of rest, from a person at rest. We die to anxiety-ridden religion so that we can truly bear fruit for God (Rom. 7:4). This is the profound paradox of spiritual productivity.

So the true gospel in all its potency is both *simple* and spiritually *restful*. Experiencing this rest doesn't take that much learning, but it may take a great deal of *un*learning. Underneath all the layers of religiosity that we've added over the years, our God has already adorned the halls of our heart with his exuberant love. We may simply need to peel away those layers of restless rhetoric in order to gaze at the full splendor of God's grace.

During our journey together, we'll travel against the grain. We'll fend off some misguided Christian jargon and some double-talk that is popular today. Your beliefs may get shaken up a bit. But together, we'll endeavor to ditch the guilt and find the real freedom and relaxation that Jesus talked about, the kind you've always longed for.

Why I Wrote This Book

"Get busy for God. He needs you!"

This appears to be the mantra of so many in the Christian world today. Indeed, this might spur us to fanatical service for a time, but it ultimately breeds burnout and disillusionment. This book is designed to expose the fraud of that line of thinking and to throw open the doors to a whole new way of living—living from rest.

Lots of Christians want to believe that Christianity is about rest, but how can they relax when they're bombarded with teaching that spawns spiritual anxiety? Together we'll examine the counterfeit idea that God needs us to work *for* him. You'll learn how "easy and light" can become a daily spiritual reality and how living *from* God fits perfectly with good works.

You've probably noticed that while some Christians are running themselves ragged trying to get God to like them, others seem to believe God is already satisfied with who they are, and they're just being themselves. One group experiences anxiety, while the other enjoys *rest*.

Many Christians are asking,

- Doesn't God *need* my service?
- How can I break free from thoughts that cause stress?
- Jesus promised me rest, even in this life. Is that real?

Getting answers to these questions is a key part of learning how to be yourself and enjoying your relationship with God. In this book, we'll be challenging commonly held notions about God that create unrest, demonstrating beyond any doubt that God *wants* us to rest, and exposing our spiritual enemy as the author of religious anxiety.

So if you're tired of the fluff, the double-talk, and the pretense, or if you're simply sick of living to please other people and sometimes feel like giving up and walking away, there is another way out—a scriptural way, a way of rest. *Relaxing with God* is designed to help you discover this new way of rest, abandoning religious error and rethinking *every* motivation in life.

3

Relax: There's a New Way to Live!

The idea of relaxing with God sounds nice, but how does it happen?

When most people think of relaxing, they think of *changing their circumstances*—going out to a movie, traveling to a tropical location, and so on. But with spiritual rest, it's not really about new circumstances. It's about new thoughts in the midst of those same old circumstances. And those new thoughts have to be inspired by what God calls *the new covenant*.

Here's the thing. You can't find relaxation if you try to make Jesus fit with the old way of law-based religion. We're not supposed to! Jesus is not even from the right tribe to be an Old Testament priest. He's got the wrong birth certificate, the wrong passport. Under the law, he'd have to be a Levite, of the tribe of Levi. But God rocked the Jewish world on purpose. It's no mistake that Jesus was born into the tribe of Judah. The whole point is that *when there's a change of priesthood, there must be a change in the whole law system* (Heb. 7:12).

So when we go flirting with the law, we're kidding ourselves. Look at Jesus. His birth signals a new way, with a new priesthood and a brand-new invitation to *relax* in him.

The New and Better Way

The cross and the resurrection bring us something better, a better way to relate to God (Heb. 8:6). The fact is, people in the time of the Old Testament did not have it near as good as we do. They simply didn't enjoy everything that we can enjoy today. Sure, many of them worked overtime to commit to God and really impress him. Still, the Scriptures tell us that their spiritual experience just didn't compare to what we have today (Heb. 11:39–40).

I find that shocking, and you should too!

Think about it. They went the extra mile. They were ostracized, ridiculed, beaten, tortured, and some even killed for their faith. Yet we are the ones who get to enjoy the benefits of living on *this* side of the cross. That doesn't seem fair! And I guess it's not "fair" if you're looking at it from a perspective of earning. But if you're looking at it from a free grace perspective, it means that our experience of intimate relationship with God was bought for us and given to us for free. That's humbling. That's difficult for us to swallow. Nevertheless, we're invited to something better than your favorite Old Testament hero could ever imagine (Heb. 8:6; 11:39–40).

What is this new and better way? It's a contract that God signed with himself (Heb. 7:22; 9:15). Yes, a promise he made to Jesus. The whole thing happened within the Godhead, among the Trinity. God swore to Jesus that he would be a priest of this new way forever (Heb. 7:21), and it was by these two unchangeable things—God and Jesus—that everything is different for us on this side of the cross. Because of the promise made by God to Jesus, we are anchored to a rock-solid hope in this life that Old Testament people could only dream of (Heb. 6:18–19).

What is this new promise, this new contract, this new way? Well, a quick journey through Hebrews 8 reveals this:

- The new way is about us being God's children, *even when we aren't faithful to him.*
- The new way is about God's desires being imprinted on our *hearts* and *minds.*
- The new way is about us being given *full access* to God.
- The new way is about our sins being *completely forgotten.*

So we get to wake up every day and enjoy this thing that we didn't initiate and that we don't sustain. We get to fully enjoy something that we don't deserve at all. We get to *relax* in it and simply thank God for it. That's all we *can* do!

It's like what Adam and Eve experienced in the beginning. They were created, but not until the sixth day. They showed up "late." God basically said, "Here's everything I've already made, so now enjoy it. Go out and name some animals, run around in the Garden, and enjoy every bit of its beauty, but the hard work is over." It was God's creation, not theirs. He did the work; they didn't. They simply entered the scene and said, "Wow!" and then, "Thank you."

That's basically what we get to do. We show up, on this side of the cross, with all of the work already done. We take one look at the finished work of Jesus and we agree with God that it is *good*! Then we simply choose to live in a constant state of "wow" and "thank you." That's what faith really is. Faith says "wow" and "thank you."

Under the old way of the law, it was the polar opposite. It was about the people of Israel trying their best to remain faithful servants of God. Eventually, God said, he turned away from them, because they couldn't pull it off (Heb. 8:9).

But under this new way, all of that has changed. Now, it's about the obedient work of Jesus on the cross and through the resurrection. And our outward obedience stems from what God is already working in us. Even our spiritual growth is from God, as he has rigged that too (Phil. 1:6; Col. 2:19; 2 Tim. 2:13)!

Experience the Difference!

If you've ever wondered why things seem so different in the Old Testament, *this* is why—same God, different covenant. In the Old Testament, the Spirit would come and go, falling on people for divine acts of service. Even David, a man after God's own heart, found himself begging God not to withdraw his Spirit (Ps. 51:11). But none of the New

Testament writers wrestled with maintaining God's presence. Why not?

Think about it. First, what is the only thing that caused the Spirit of God to depart from Adam and Eve? *Sin.* Second, what is the only thing that caused Jesus to say, "My God, why have you forsaken me" (Matt. 27:46)? *Sin,* as Jesus was bearing the sin of the world. Third, what is the only thing that would cause the Spirit of God to depart from you today? *Sin.*

But what did Jesus do with our sins? He took them away forever (John 1:29; Heb. 10:14). That's why the Spirit of God will never leave us.

Bam! That's the simple, logical, and liberating difference of God's new way of grace—permanent relationship, permanent indwelling by God's Spirit, no matter what. Yes, even when we commit sins, he remembers them no more (Heb. 8:12). Even when we are utterly disobedient, he remains faithful. The Holy Spirit is sealed within us, forever, and he will never leave us nor forsake us (Eph. 1:13–14; Heb. 13:5).

So what is the result of all of this supposed to be?

"Ahhhh." We breathe a big sigh of relief. We take in the splendor of the new covenant and celebrate with amazement. We *relax* in the grand beauty of God's perfect promises.

All of the religious stress is just plain unnecessary. That old way is not for today. And nobody (I mean, nobody!) could ever make it work (Acts 13:39; Rom. 3:28; Gal. 2:16; 3:11). It was a weak way that is now obsolete and useless (Heb. 7:18; 8:13). A brief trip through Hebrews 7–10, and anybody can see that.

Still, it seems like many of today's church leaders are blind to the new covenant focus. But look, there's really only *one* thing to minister—the new covenant—and nothing else (2 Cor. 3:6). When churches start ministering anything else, it inevitably leads to some form of law-based living. Yeah, it might be well-adjusted, religious law. It might be law with a little Christian hat on top. But if it's the message of "do more" and "be more" and then God will respond in turn, that's law. Law is any belief system in which God responds *after* we initiate with our good behavior. So it might not be 613 Jewish laws blatantly staring us in the face, but it's still law nonetheless. Law is an attitude, a spiritual mindset of "earning" and "achieving." And a law mentality will never, ever allow us to *relax* with God.

So if you're looking for real change in your experience, it's going to involve ditching that whole "have-to" mentality and the religious rules that go with it. Are you willing to consider God's new way of "want to" (Col. 2:20–23) to see what it might mean for you personally?

It's *All* Inspired!

Now, I can hear some people thinking, "He's saying that we should tear the Old Testament out of our Bibles!" Well, I'm not saying that at all. I'm saying that the whole Bible is God's inspired Word, but we can enjoy a nice shrimp cocktail just like anybody else. And I'm saying there's no issue with Friday night emails or Saturday yard work either (disobeying the Sabbath). But isn't the book of Leviticus the inspired Word of God too? Yeah, sure it is! But like me, you've already figured out that living on this side of the cross with a New Testament mentality *changes the way we view the Old Testament law.*

So let's be transparent about our relationship with the law. Let's not mince words. Yes, the Old Testament law is the Word of God. But that old covenant is now obsolete and has no glory at all in comparison with the new covenant (2 Cor. 3:10; Heb. 8:13). Not to mention, if you're a Gentile (non-Jew), then you were never even given the law to start with! Ephesians 2 says those of us who are Gentiles had no hope and no covenant. We were never invited to the law.

Think on that one for a minute. There's a load of debate out there about law and grace: Should we adopt *some* of the law? Don't we need a balance of law and grace? And the truth is that 99 percent of the people debating the issue are Gentiles. *For us, it's the new covenant or nothing at all.*

So let's enjoy everything from Genesis to Revelation, knowing it's all inspired. But let's also recognize that there's a surprise ending to the story—the cross and the resurrection! This surprise ending inspires us to go back and *reinterpret* the beginning of the story in light of all that has now been revealed. So let's look at the old covenant, which is now obsolete, through the lens of the new covenant. There's simply no other way to fully relax with God.

PART 1

RELAX IN THE FINALITY OF THE CROSS

4

You're Dead
to Law-Based Religion

The Jewish law is just one flavor of law-based living. It's a strict and in fact perfect standard given by God to Israel long ago. But like any system of strict rules, law only shows who the hypocrites are. That's all it's designed to do. Law crumbles religious dreams and shuts everybody up, revealing they are prisoners of sin. The Bible reveals that living under the law is like living under a curse (Rom. 2:21–24; 3:19–20; Gal. 3:10, 19–24)!

Still, what we see today is preachers and teachers lining up at the buffet line of law in order to select their favorite foods. Some pick tithing. Others pick the Sabbath. Even when those two aren't chosen, they still pick the nine "moral laws" about lying, stealing, coveting, and so on and throw those on our plates. Little do they realize how much their selections are going to weigh us all down. And it seems *so* innocent. After all, what's wrong with having a few moral laws over you to keep you on the right road?

Apparently, when you invite the Ten Commandments into your life, you're inviting condemnation. Now, I'm not making this up. Crack your Bible open to 2 Corinthians 3:7 and see what it says—that law is a ministry of condemnation and death. Then ask yourself, "Which part of the law is Paul talking about here?" The answer is . . . (drum roll) . . . the Ten Commandments! Yeah, he's specifically talking about the part of the law that was *written on stone*. And we all know that *only* the Big Ten were written on stone. So the Ten Commandments themselves are a ministry of condemnation and death. There's just no two ways about it.

But wait, there's more. In Romans 7, we find that "apart from the law, sin was dead" (v. 8). Apparently, if we're going to find freedom from sin's grip, it's got to happen *apart* from law. Now, that's not with *a part of* the law. That's *apart* from law. Big difference.

Again, as you read Romans 7:8, ask yourself, "Which part of the law is Paul talking about here?" Again, the answer is . . . (drum roll, please) . . . the Ten Commandments! How do we know? Well, he's talking about coveting and how being under the law resulted in coveting of every kind for him. The "do not covet" law is one of the Big Ten. So here again we're seeing that inviting the Ten Commandments into your life is the same as inviting sin to be alive and thrive in your life. Only *apart* from the Ten Commandments is sin dead.

It's All or Nothing

Weird. Counterintuitive. Something we'd never dream up.

Yeah, if we were going to concoct some religion for the world to follow, we'd be sure to include a long list of rules to "motivate" everyone. But God announces the startling reality that under rules, people try their best to crank out good behavior and end up with egg on their faces, every single time (Rom. 5:20; 7:5, 8; 2 Cor. 3:7; Col. 2:20–23).

Here's the other thing: we're not allowed to stand at the buffet line of law and start picking and choosing anyway. No, it's all or nothing, not a little here and a little there. Both James and Galatians tell us that if you don't keep the whole law, then you're under its curse (James 2:10; Gal. 3:10).

Even if you only mess up in one tiny way, you're toast. That's the law for you. So it's not about the Big Ten, or the Big Nine if we omit Sabbath observance. No, it's about 613 laws in all, if you're *really* going to go there. Otherwise, abandon the sinking ship and hop on the grace train!

After all, our flirtation with any portion of the law reveals our total disrespect for its perfection. Only those who opt for grace truly respect the perfect and impossible standard of the *whole* law. Everyone else is just kidding themselves.

I'm not sure the God of the universe can shout it any more clearly: we died to the law so that we can finally bear real fruit for him! Anything else is a mirage of self-improvement. Christ brings a dramatic end to the law for us. And if we go back and choose law after being married to Christ, then we insult the Son of God himself (Rom.

7:4; 10:4; Gal. 5:2–4). We're cheating on Jesus! So why in the world would any of us think that our own modern-day flavor of law-living is any less offensive or any more effective?

Now, I'm not saying that the law has passed away or anything, so don't go all Matthew 5 on me. I think we're all aware that the law has *not* died. Jesus himself said that not even the slightest bit of the law would ever pass away until heaven and earth disappear (Matt. 5:17–19), and last I checked they're still around. So the law did not die, but we died *to* the law. Our role now is to act dead to it, because we *are* dead to it. It's simply not for us as believers.

So yes, the law is still around, and it's not going anywhere anytime soon. It's holy and perfect in every way (Rom. 7:12). And it's super useful in pointing out the grime on the face of humanity. It's just not any good at wiping it off!

Now, the law certainly isn't dead. It's very much alive and can initially point us to our need for Jesus (Gal. 3:24). And if we didn't grow up around a whole lot of Moses, then it's our conscience that convicts us (Rom. 2:15). But let's be clear: *once we are placed in Christ at salvation, we completely die to the law and resurrect in Christ, led by the Spirit, with no need for the law in our lives* (Rom. 6:14; 7:12; Gal. 3:23–25; 5:18; 1 Tim. 1:7–9).

That's a big deal!

I don't know why this topic has historically been so debated. It's really pretty simple, not complicated. Maybe that is why so many do miss it. We want to make things sophisticated. We want to be experts in the intricacies of religion, so we slice and dice God's law so that we can get it exactly the way we like it. Then we say that *part* of it is for us. We select the Ten. Or we omit the Sabbath and make it the Nine. Or we throw tithing into the mix, and it's, "Look, Ma, a new set of Ten!"

But here's the way it's supposed to be: we are dead to the law (Rom. 7:4); we are not under the law (Rom. 6:14; Gal. 5:18); Christ is the end of the law for us (Rom. 10:4). Plain and simple.

Yet not getting this is a *very* old problem. We see it in Galatians when Paul started with the name-calling: "You foolish Galatians!" (3:1). His point was that this thing should be simple for all of us. We're foolish to make it so complicated. Our relationship with the law is entirely over; we're dead to it, period (Rom. 7:4; Gal. 3:25).

We serve God in a totally different way—in freedom. We can afford to live in a law-free environment, because we're led by God's Spirit. This isn't some life that is mystical and far off. It too is simple. It's simple to be motivated and inspired by faith in a Person living within us rather than having to keep 613 laws in mind all the time (Rom. 7:6; Gal. 5:13, 18). Talk about a headache!

What about Behavior?

Still, there are laws of *some* kind within Christianity. After all, we know that God's desires were etched on the lining of our spiritual hearts. But a brief tour through the epistle of 1 John reveals that those laws involve believing in Jesus and loving others. In short, *believe* and *love* (1 John 3:23). These are the laws written on our hearts, not 613 laws of

Judaism. John says that these commands are "not burdensome" (1 John 5:3).

Even the idea of "love your neighbor as yourself" is *not precisely* what's written on our hearts. No, that command was named as one of the two greatest commands *in the law* (see Matt. 22:36–40). So that's still the law. In contrast, what is on our hearts today is the "new command" that Jesus brought in: loving others even as he loves us (John 13:34; Rom. 13:8–10; 1 John 3:23). That's the new way—to soak in his love for us and to transmit it to others. Does that sound burdensome to you?

Someone might say, "C'mon, there's a ton of behavior verses in the New Testament, so let's not pretend like there aren't any rules for us to follow."

Well, there are loads of behavior verses, for sure. But I guess it comes down to how you view them. To see the difference between Old Testament law and New Testament instruction, ask yourself: What if I don't obey? What are the consequences of my failure to obey? Old covenant law and new covenant grace will give you two very different answers to that one!

The old covenant set out severe punishments for disobedience under the law, including even death. But under the new covenant, the punishment has been taken in full by Christ and his death on the cross (Rom. 8:1; Heb. 9:28; 1 Pet. 2:23). After all, that's why he died, right? To take on our punishment, to pay the price in full, in our place. So when we fail to live by God's instruction under the new covenant, we still reap earthly consequences, but God Almighty is not heaping punishment on us. Remember, if he were, the wages of sin would be death for us, not merely a slap on the wrist. No, it would be death that God would be doling out. So thank God that Jesus died in our place, and thank God for this new way of grace!

Obviously, it's very wise to listen to God's instruction. When we do, we enjoy the privilege of transmitting his life and displaying his divine nature to those around us. We also avoid a load of wasted time and effort going in the wrong direction (Rom. 6:21; 1 Cor. 10:23).

If we are foolish enough to choose another path in a given moment, God goes right along with us. He is in us no matter what, and he picks up the pieces with us after we fall. He never leaves us.

That's the main difference between the in-and-out, here-and-gone relationship with God that some are pushing today and the radical, new way of grace we're called to enjoy.

The Big Picture

We are dead to the law. We are not under the law. We are not supervised by the law. Christ is the end of the law for us. Our guide is the Holy Spirit, for "if you are led by the Spirit, you are not under the law" (Gal. 5:18). This verse is *not* about salvation. No, it's about what is *leading* and *guiding* our behavior. We are led by God's Spirit, not the law.

The law is not the source, and the law is not the goal. Knowing Jesus is our source for upright living. And knowing Jesus is our ultimate goal too. Some Christian teachers claim that now that we have the Holy Spirit living within us,

41

he will help us keep the law. But nothing could be further from the truth! The righteous standards of the law have already been "fully met" by Christ Jesus (Rom. 8:3–4), so we don't need to meet them! In short, God is not helping us avoid pork chops or shrimp cocktail; and God is not helping us stay work-free on the Sabbath (one of the Ten) either. Yes, God causes us to bear the fruit of his Spirit, but the law is not the source, and *the law is not the goal.*

Recall that many Christians in the early church were Gentiles and thus had never heard of Moses and had no idea what those 613 law requirements even were. They were only concerned with bearing the fruit of the Spirit. Jesus Christ was their *source*, and knowing him and his fruit was their *goal*. It should be the same for us today!

So let's face it: *those who claim we are free from the ceremonial law but are still guided by the moral law want Jesus for his blood but not for his life.* Still, no matter what they might say, the fact remains: we are led by the Spirit, not the law (Gal. 5:18).

5

You're Totally Forgiven

Let's be candid. The whole Old Testament way was messy, gross, and barbaric at times. As early as the giving of the law, Moses sprinkled blood all over the scroll and then—get this—all over the people (Heb. 9:19).

That's one church service I'd rather miss!

But that bloody, messy system was established for a reason. Like it or not, it signals something very important for us—God's blood economy. We read in Hebrews 9:22 that there is no forgiveness without blood being shed. Now, what's the takeaway for us? Well, it's still the same today—there's no forgiveness without bloodshed. So, connecting the dots, here's the big deal:

- Only *blood* brings forgiveness.
- Jesus shed his blood *once*, and it needs no repeat.
- We were forgiven *once* for *all* our sins.

43

Let me say it another way: Jesus isn't dying daily, so we aren't being forgiven daily, little by little (Heb. 9:25–29). There won't be any new portions of God's forgiveness coming our way at any point in the future, because no more blood will ever be shed for our sins. In other words, it's finished. (Sound familiar? See John 19:30.) *We've already got all the forgiveness we're ever going to need!*

This is why Hebrews contrasts what Jesus accomplished ("once for all") with the never-ending way of the Old Testament. The writer exclaims: "[Jesus] does not need to offer sacrifices *day after day*, first for his own sins, and then for the sins of the people. He sacrificed for their sins *once for all* when he offered himself" (Heb. 7:27). So, it's simple. One sacrifice for all sins means we're forgiven, not day after day, not little by little, but *once . . .* and *for all*!

But inhabitants of planet Earth operate very differently from God. Here, among us Homo sapiens, we want to see sorrow in the heart and apologies on the lips. Then and only then will we dole out that coveted phrase, "I forgive you." In contrast, God's way has always been about blood, not words. As early as Leviticus 9, we see Aaron needing to go to an altar and make blood sacrifices for himself and all of the Israelites. But Hebrews reveals that even though those sacrifices were carried out over and over, year after year, they *never took away* any sins at all (Heb. 10:4, 11). They only *covered* (atoned for) sins, without taking them away. It is only through Christ Jesus that sins are taken away. Jesus is the only way that any human is ever "cleansed once for all" (Heb. 10:2).

The complete takeaway of sins was something never experienced under the law (Heb. 10:4, 11). That's why John the Baptist was so excited when he shouted that Jesus was the Lamb of God "who *takes away* the sin of the world" (John 1:29). That's why the writer of Hebrews was so thrilled that Christ had been sacrificed once to "take away" sins (9:28). Such a feat—a total takeaway—had never been accomplished before!

Do We Really Get It?

Still, as great as that feat was, it seems like we're just not getting it. The Catholic goes to Mass in order to "get" forgiveness when the bread and the wine of the Eucharist are supposedly transformed into the body and blood of Jesus inside them. In preparation for the Mass, they might talk to a priest in a confession booth. Somewhere between their words of confession and their ritual meal, they believe they're getting cleansed—weekly, monthly, or, for the less dedicated, at least at Easter and Christmas.

Now, the Protestant might believe that he does much better. He chuckles at the idea of some human priest or some ceremony being necessary for him to obtain God's forgiveness today. He says, "I go to God directly, and when I confess my sins to God, he forgives me and cleanses me every time I ask."

Here's the thing. *Both* of these systems ignore the "once for all" takeaway of our sins. In fact, both the Catholic and the Protestant systems described above incite *more bondage* for us than the Jewish law ever did!

I realize that's a strong statement, but think about it. At least the Jewish man went to the Day of Atonement only *once per year*, where he got 365 days of sins covered. But the Catholic and the Protestant are working much harder, seeking to obtain forgiveness on a weekly or monthly basis (Catholic) at the Mass or, even worse, on an individual *sin-by-sin* basis (Protestant) through direct confessions to God!

Neither the Catholic nor the Protestant in these scenarios is trusting in the "once for all" sacrifice of Jesus Christ that needs no repeat. The bottom line is that it doesn't matter whether you go to a human priest or directly to God himself to "get forgiven" progressively (little by little); the point is that *Jesus doesn't dole out forgiveness on a one-by-one basis* (Heb. 9:25).

You either have the "once for all" or nothing at all.

What Are You Signing Up For?

Realize what you're signing up for if you disregard the "once for all" forgiveness offered in Christ. Imagine if it were up to you to remember every sin and to confess every sin in order to be forgiven by God. What if you forgot to confess one? Imagine if you were only forgiven of sins that you clearly repented of and began to overcome in your life. What if you died before getting a sin issue resolved? The whole thing leads to stress and fear, not relaxing in the finished work of Jesus. It's got to be about the blood of Jesus alone. Nothing else makes any sense!

It's not our memory, our many words, or any ceremony that makes us forgiven. Remember that there is *no blood*

46

being shed in those moments, and only blood brings forgiveness. So it's the one-time sacrifice of Jesus that made us forgiven, and it is finished (John 19:30). It's over. You are a totally forgiven person.

While religious systems might tell us to get right and get clean with God over and over again, the new covenant way of grace reveals that Jesus was the *hilastērion* (propitiation; 1 John 2:2), meaning "the gift that satisfies completely." And if God is satisfied with the sacrifice of his Son, then who are we to argue with him?

This is precisely why passages in the New Testament that discuss our forgiveness express it in *past tense*. Whether in Ephesians, or Colossians, or Hebrews, or 1 John, many passages say God "forgave" us all our sins and that we "have been" forgiven (Eph. 4:32; Col. 2:13; Heb. 10:18; 1 John 2:12). It's past tense because nothing new is going to happen.

Think about it: all of your sins were in the future when Christ died. There's no distinction between sins *before* salvation and sins *after* salvation when it comes to the blood of Jesus Christ. Imagine if there were! Does the gospel actually become *less powerful* to you *after* you're saved? Do sins after salvation somehow get treated differently when it comes to the cross? If that were true, the best strategy would be to wait to get saved just before you breathe your last breath. At least then you wouldn't have to "manage your cleansing" very long before you met your Maker.

The whole scenario is absurd, and so is that belief system.

Some Thoughts on Asking and Sorrow

The phrases "ask forgiveness" and "ask for forgiveness" do not appear even once in any New Testament epistle. In fact, while these phrases appear about a dozen times in the Qur'an, they don't show up anywhere in the Bible at all! While it's a very religious move to ask for forgiveness, the plain fact is that God works within a blood-based economy, so it's not about asking.

But when some hear that asking for forgiveness is unnecessary and unbiblical, it raises all kinds of red flags in their minds. Some presume that not asking for forgiveness means eliminating all sorrow over sins. Let me be the first to say that *sorrow over a sin committed is normal and expected in the Christian life.*

What should we do when we sin? Stop. Turn from it. Act differently (Eph. 4:28). Seek repair with those we've hurt (Rom. 12:18; James 5:16). Still, in all of this, we don't have to *ask* for God to forgive us. Instead, we simply recall that our confidence is in the once-for-all sacrifice of his Son, and we *thank* him that we are forgiven people. That is how we truly honor the finished work of Jesus!

Discerning the Double-Talkers

Now that we've established that sorrow over sins is healthy, you can breathe a sigh of relief, and we can address some related issues. We've seen that the idea that believers should ask for forgiveness essentially stems from attributing imperfect, human characteristics to God. And aside from the Lord's Prayer, which I will address in the next chapter, no passage in Scripture even remotely communicates that we need to *ask* God for forgiveness. The reason that requesting cleansing is absent from all the epistles is simple. In contrast to humans, who typically require an apology before forgiving, God issues forgiveness based on one type of currency—blood. And the requirement for our forgiveness and cleansing from God has already been met on the cross. So there's nothing we can *do* to make our forgiveness any more real than it already is right now!

But if you've spent any time in theology books, you know that some of the "experts" will tell you that we Christians are forgiven for all of our sins "positionally, but not relationally." Or maybe you've heard that we're forgiven "in God's heavenly bookkeeping but not on Earth." Still others say our total forgiveness is "patriarchal" or "forensic" (we've got Sherlock Holmes involved in this?) but not "actual" until we confess or ask forgiveness.

This terminology makes me want to laugh and cry all at the same time.

Why all the convoluted double-talk? Not one of these expressions appears anywhere in the Bible! So what is the motive behind it all? Well, there's actually one good motive here, I believe. (Yes, I'm giving the benefit of the doubt.) Here's the likely motive: these "experts" don't want us to keep on sinning. And that is a healthy concern. But where they err is in *holding our forgiveness hostage to non-biblical terms and ideas*. That's no way to motivate Christians. But they think that by casting doubt on our forgiveness (in the "earthly" realm), they can motivate Christians to stay on the right road. In short, they're afraid. They're afraid that if total forgiveness is taught with all clarity, it will only lead to more sinning. (Note that this is a very old and tired concern addressed long ago in Romans 6:1–2.)

But here's a news flash for you: *God never motivates us by withholding his forgiveness*! He motivates us by giving us a new heart filled with new desires and then telling us who we actually are. He lets us know that we are dead to sin, alive to him, and not made for anything short of expressing his Spirit (Rom. 6:1–6).

Of course, it's perfectly fine to tell Christians that when we sin, we are quenching (not expressing) God's Spirit (1 Thess. 5:19) and that we will end up unfulfilled. It's also perfectly biblical to tell Christians that when we sin, we can expect earthly consequences for our choices (Gal. 6:8). But to tell Christians they are *not forgiven* until they meet some condition? Well, that's just insulting to the blood of Jesus!

Think about this one: Even under the law, when a Jewish person celebrated the Day of Atonement, the blood from those bulls and goats led to *actual* and *earthly* relief from guilt for 365 days worth of sins. So what are we saying if we tell Christians that the blood of Christ himself did not give them a lifetime of real forgiveness here and now? Is the blood of Christ *less* powerful than that of animals?

When it comes to forgiveness, some theologians speak of "claiming it" or "appropriating it" or "making it real in our experience" on a daily basis. Despite their popularity, these terms aren't actually biblical expressions related to forgiveness either. If we're in Christ, the reality is that we're totally forgiven people, whether we fully understand it or not. Realizing the truth simply allows us to cease the restless activity of trying to get forgiven and to instead express our gratitude to God. This is the act of true faith that brings a smile to his face (Heb. 13:15).

6

It's Not about You

Some latch on to a few passages of Scripture as so-called proof that we aren't totally forgiven yet. Armed with these passages, they claim that there's still something for us Christians to *do* in order to get more forgiven or cleansed before God. So in this chapter, we'll look at a few of these weapons of choice.

In Matthew 6:12, we see Jesus praying a prayer that includes the request, "forgive us." So should we get busy praying that same sort of prayer, asking for forgiveness over and over, throughout our lives as Christians?

In that same chapter, Jesus himself warned against mindless repetition of prayers, yet some turn right around and recite Jesus's prayer in Matthew 6 as if it were the "gold standard" without much concern for the audience and the context.

Remember that Jesus didn't simply pray, "forgive us." No, he specifically prayed, "forgive us . . . *as we also have forgiven those. . . .*" (Matt. 6:12). In other words, he was saying that his disciples should ask God to forgive them *in the same way* and *to the same degree* that they had forgiven other people. Ouch. Now, that's a deadly prayer!

Not sure that Jesus actually meant to communicate a conditional forgiveness? Well, here's his conclusion right after the prayer, which screams loud and clear: "For *if you forgive other people* when they sin against you, your heavenly Father will *also* forgive you. But *if you do not forgive others* their sins, your Father will *not* forgive your sins" (Matt. 6:14–15).

We don't have to guess at Jesus's meaning, because he spells it out for us. It's clear that Jesus was saying that getting forgiveness from God was contingent upon them forgiving others.

Now, is that the gospel? Is that the new covenant way of grace? Certainly not! The new covenant way is found in Ephesians 4:32 and Colossians 3:13. They both say to forgive others because God *already* forgave us. This is very different from forgiving others in order to earn our own forgiveness from God!

So why does Matthew 6 seem to say something different about forgiveness than what we find in Ephesians and Colossians? Well, that's an easy one. One passage demonstrates the futility of prayers for forgiveness *before* the "once for all" sacrifice on Calvary. Meanwhile, the other two passages proclaim the truth that it is finished, so now pass it on to others! One scenario is *before* the cross; the other is *after* the cross. After all, when it comes to forgiveness, wouldn't you think that the cross would dramatically change things? It certainly does!

There's a reason we don't find one single instance of asking for forgiveness in the New Testament epistles. Jesus never intended us to mindlessly and ritualistically repeat the prayer in Matthew 6. The whole purpose of that prayer was to expose how despondent anyone would be under a system of being forgiven only to the same degree that they've forgiven others.

Jesus told the Jews of his day to cut off their hands (Matt. 5:30), pluck out their eyes (Matt. 5:29), be perfect like God (Matt. 5:48), and sell everything they had (Matt. 19:21). Their hearts sank at his words, knowing that if that was God's true standard, then they had no hope (Matt. 19:22). His prayer in Matthew 6 was uttered for the very same purpose—to show that forgiveness *cannot be earned* and that God's forgiveness of us must be *greater* than our forgiveness of others, or we are in serious trouble!

The Foot-Washing Fetish

Yeah, but aren't we 90 percent forgiven and still in need of daily "foot washing" touch-ups? John 13 presents a conversation between Peter and Jesus that has sparked a lot of ideas about our forgiveness not being total yet. A popular interpretation of this passage is that Peter needed to bathe that morning (a symbol of getting "positionally" forgiven at salvation), but he also needed regular foot washing (a symbol of getting daily touch-ups of more forgiveness). So this popular teaching neglects the truth of our once-for-all cleansing in Christ and proposes a daily, self-induced foot-washing fetish of asking for more forgiveness.

But when examined closely, this conversation between Peter and Jesus gives little opportunity for such a skewed interpretation. In this passage, Jesus has one main objective—to demonstrate the idea of *servanthood*. This becomes obvious as Jesus concludes his teaching:

> When he had finished washing their feet, he put on his clothes and returned to his place. "Do you understand what I have done for you?" he asked them. "You call me 'Teacher' and 'Lord,' and rightly so, for that is what I am. Now that I, your Lord and Teacher, have washed your feet, *you also should wash one another's feet.* I have set you *an example* that you should do as I have done for you." (vv. 12–15)

Where did Jesus go with the foot-washing event? He wasn't concerned with the concept of forgiveness. Instead, he was making a point about *serving one another.*

Now, Jesus did say, "Unless I wash you, you have no part with me" (v. 8). Whether or not this even relates to forgiveness is debatable. He may have essentially been saying, "If you do not let me serve you, you have no part with me." It takes humility to be served by Jesus. It takes an attitude of submission to let him work in our lives.

But even if Jesus were alluding to the cleansing work of the cross here, it's important to point out that Jesus only washed Peter's feet *once.* Moreover, Jesus certainly did not bathe Peter that morning! The idea that Peter's morning bath symbolizes one act of Christ and that foot washing symbolizes a second act of Christ is preposterous. There are no grounds for making that intellectual leap.

Jesus makes no mention of any cleansing beyond feet. It is Peter who tries to bring out the body wash. But Jesus halts Peter's eagerness to get his whole body cleaned by basically saying, "Look, I'm washing feet, Peter, nothing more. You already had a bath this morning" (see v. 10).

So Jesus washes only feet. He performs this act *only once* on each disciple. In that era, foot washing was a custom carried out by servants. When performed by a master on his followers, it was a stunning countercultural example of humble servanthood that raised eyebrows, including Peter's. Then Jesus encouraged his disciples to serve one another in the same way that he had served them.

This conversation was intended to illustrate radical, humble servanthood, not to advocate a system for daily spiritual "touch-ups." There are simply no grounds for building a two-tiered theology involving "positional" forgiveness at salvation and then a further need for daily "foot washings." So we can drop the foot-washing fetish and just relax.

Understanding 1 John 1:9

But wait, we're not done! I saved the most popular passage in the you're-not-forgiven arsenal for last.

First John 1:9 says, "*If we confess our sins*, he is faithful and just and will forgive us our sins and purify us from all unrighteousness." So what if we don't confess our sins? I mean, what if we forget one? Does God not forgive us and not cleanse us? This verse has caused more confusion about the finished work of Christ than any other in the history of the church.

Here's a remarkable idea: In order to understand the true meaning of verse 9, what if we look to verses 8 and 10 to help us out?

Context. There's just nothing like it to bring clarity.

Two thousand years ago there were people saying that they were without sin (v. 8) and that they had never sinned (v. 10). These people did not have the truth in them (v. 8), nor did God's Word have any place in their lives (v. 10). In other words, *they were not yet saved.* John briefly addresses this group of people in his letter. He says that if we (any one of us!) think that we have no sin or that we have never sinned, then we are totally deceiving ourselves and calling God a liar!

Imagine someone saying to you, "Sin? What sin? There's no such thing as sin in my life. I've never sinned." What would you conclude about a person like that? Are they a Christian? No way! After all, the first step to becoming a Christian is *admitting that you're a sinner in need of a Savior*!

Notice that John says that he's addressing this group's false beliefs "so that you also may have fellowship with us. And our fellowship is with the Father and with his Son, Jesus Christ" (1 John 1:3). Some of these people he's writing to do not yet have any fellowship with Christians or with the Father and Son. Why not? Because they are still *unbelievers* who are going so far as to even deny the reality of sin. John writes them to correct their belief system and invite them to the truth "so that you also may have fellowship with us" (v. 3).

Real Christians have the truth in them forever (2 John 1:1–2). But the people John is addressing in the first chapter of 1 John do *not* have the truth in them yet (v. 8). How could they? They're not even ready to admit their sinfulness! That's why John is essentially telling them, "Hey, if any of us is saying crazy things about sinless performance, there's a simple solution—just admit your sins. Then God will forgive and cleanse you of *all* unrighteousness."

It's an invitation to admit sin, to believe, and to receive forgiveness of *all* sins.

Notice that it's "all unrighteousness" that we get cleansed of (v. 9), not one sin here and one sin there. It's not little by little. It's once for all. So 1 John 1:9 is an invitation for the crazy sin denier to come to his senses and to receive salvation, which of course includes *total* forgiveness.

I find it absolutely ridiculous (and insulting to Jesus) that many of us today have used this passage as a bar-of-soap sin cleanser for daily washings before God. That's not the point at all. Daily, verbal conversations with God about our sin struggles are healthy and good, but they don't wash us and cleanse us. The blood of Jesus did that, once for all!

Once we see the true meaning of this passage and the others clarified here, we can begin to truly relax in the finished work of Jesus.

Yes, you can relax, because *it's really not about you*!

7

It Really Is Finished

Some brand this biblical teaching of "once for all" forgiveness as being anti-confession or anti-repentance. First, let me say that it's *not* anti-confession; it's just pro-Calvary! Sure, confession (admitting our struggles) is healthy, but *it doesn't make any new portion of forgiveness come our way.* We confess our sins because it's part of being honest and open with God and with trusted friends. We confess our sins because it's a way of speaking the truth about our current struggles so that people can pray for us (James 5:16). But we don't confess our sins so that Jesus will somehow shed more blood and then zap us with a new portion of cleansing. That's simply not happening.

Most who oppose the "once for all" forgiveness message taught in the Bible do not take the time to understand the main point. Yes, there are plenty of reasons to admit our wrongdoing and to turn from sin and to act differently, but getting more forgiveness from God is not one of them! Clearly, we don't have to remember and confess every sin we've ever committed in order to be forgiven by God. After all, we can't even remember every sin we've committed! No, it's not about our memory and our words. It's about the blood of Jesus and his once-for-all sacrifice. But holding to this belief does not even remotely imply that we should continue sinning or neglect admitting our sins.

So if by confession we mean the biblical definition—*homo logos* (basically, "agreeing with God")—then why not agree with God about sins? In fact, why not agree with God about *everything*? And clearly the Bible tells us to turn away from sinful attitudes and actions and choose to act differently, not letting sin reign in our lives.

That's a no-brainer.

The point is not what we don't have to do. The point is what Jesus *did*—he took away our sins, once for all! So we admit our struggles to God and to others who will pray for us, but *not in order to be more forgiven by God.*

That's the point.

Is This Anti-Repentance?

This new covenant message of "once for all" forgiveness is not anti-repentance. As far as repentance goes, the word simply means to change your mind. It ultimately means that we decide to think and act differently—to make a 180-degree turn. Any Christian who has read much of the Bible knows that God is no fan of sin. He hates sin. He doesn't want his children to sin. So the proper response to sin is to do that 180-degree turn and get away from it, to think and act differently.

Again, that's a no-brainer.

So I'm amazed that some people misinterpret the message of "once for all" forgiveness to mean that we ignore agreeing with God or ignore God's counsel and discipline. That's absurd. We are to be honest and open with God and trusted friends about our struggles. And we're designed, as new creations who are dead to sin and alive to God, to reject sin and act differently. But *neither of these makes us more forgiven*. That's the point. Only blood brings forgiveness, and Jesus will never die again. So we are forgiven people!

Consider this: Isn't there some other reason to admit when you're wrong and to turn from it? Is "getting forgiveness" the only reason we can imagine for admitting our wrongdoing? I can think of so many better, biblical reasons to admit my wrongdoing and turn from it: because I'm dead to sin and not made for it (Rom. 6:2); because I'm alive to God and designed for so much more (Rom. 6:11); and because sin hurts people and never fulfills (Rom. 6:21), just to name a few. Work your way through the second half of Romans 6, and you'll see that those are the biblical reasons to turn away from sinful attitudes and actions.

The book of 2 Corinthians reveals that there's a godly sorrow that leads to our turning from sin and acting differently (7:10), and both Ephesians and 1 Thessalonians say that God invests in our attitudes and actions and that his Spirit is quenched (rather than expressed) and grieved (concerned over us) when we do damage to ourselves and those around us (Eph. 4:30; 1 Thess. 5:19). God wants the best for us! But "getting more and more forgiveness from God" is not any reason to confess or repent. Only Christ's blood achieved that, so let's not spit on the sacrifice of Jesus. God remembers our sins no more (Heb. 8:12; 10:17). Let's go with God's opinion on this one.

What should we do after we've sinned? Stop sinning, act differently, and reconcile with others who have been hurt. That's plain and obvious. But we don't have to somehow "get right with God." Many times, it seems like we're focused on getting right with God instead of getting right with those we've actually harmed!

Consider those who were stealing in Ephesus. What was Paul's solution for them? Stop stealing, get a job, work with your hands, and give to those in need (Eph. 4:28). But Paul never said a thief should get down on the ground and grovel for forgiveness. Romans 5:1 says we *already* have peace *with God*, but Romans 12:18 tells us to live at peace *with people*.

So which chapter are you living in? Are you chasing after peace with God, which you already have, or are you living *from* peace with God and now seeking peace with others?

We should turn from sinful activity and depend on God's Spirit for real change in our attitudes and actions. But no amount of "turning from our sins" causes Jesus to die again. And since forgiveness comes through blood alone, no amount of ongoing repentance makes us more forgiven. Instead, here's the plain reality: "By *one* offering He has *perfected for all time* those who are sanctified" (Heb. 10:14 NASB).

Now, if anyone says this total forgiveness teaching is going "light on sin," it's not. It's actually going *heavy on sin.* The wages of sin is *death*, not God being hacked off at you for five minutes until you apologize, like some suggest. So sin is serious, with death as the only just penalty. But Jesus died, so he paid that penalty in full, and that's the message of the gospel.

Some say that this much grace is too radical, so it simply can't be right. Well, I'm not sure how you tone down grace. Romans 11:6 tells us that if you add any work to it, then grace is no longer grace! Some call this total forgiveness message "hypergrace." Well, yeah, I'm pretty hyper about it, and you should be too! Then others say it's "cheap grace." Well, it's better than cheap. It's free. Yes, it did cost Jesus his life, so it was very expensive at the start. But now that it has been purchased and paid for in full, this gift of total forgiveness is much better than cheap. It's absolutely free!

Free Fellowship Too!

The *fellowship* is free too, by the way. People talk about fellowship like it's a connection with God that comes and goes with our behavior. No way. In the Bible, if you're a new creation, a child of God, then your Father remains "in fellowship" with you at all times (1 Cor. 1:9; 2 Cor. 13:14; 1 John 1:7).

"Out of fellowship" would mean that you were lost, spiritually dead, without hope. You're either in fellowship with God, connected to him and therefore saved (1 Cor. 6:17), or you are out of fellowship with God, disconnected from him and therefore lost. There is no in-between state. There's no going in and out of fellowship. That's fiction.

That's just somebody taking a term out of the Bible and redefining it to their liking. The truth is that our fellowship is unshakable and unbreakable because of what Jesus did, not because of what we are doing. Otherwise, we'd be out of fellowship every time we sinned!

Imagine going in and out of fellowship all day, every day. What a way to develop a neurosis! You'd end up so neurotic that nobody in their right mind would want to be like you. Then we talk about witnessing? Would this be our witness? "Become a Christian and ride this roller coaster of performance-driven connection with God like me!"

I'm sure they'd be lining up at your door to hear the "Good News."

The reality is that if we're going to sin, then we have to sin *while* we are in fellowship, firmly connected to God. That's why it's simply not as much fun as it used to be! Yes, there are all kinds of consequences on planet Earth when we sin. If we sin in the workplace, we might lose our job. If we sin in the home, our spouse might leave us. If we sin in our private lives, we might find ourselves addicted to something. Those are *earthly consequences* that we can bring on ourselves. But that's very different from God withdrawing his presence, causing us to lose fellowship.

No, if we were going to get what was coming to us, it'd be "the needle," as a friend of mine likes to put it. It wouldn't be ten minutes or ten days of being "out of fellowship" until we shape up. No, it'd be death, because no lesser punishment would suffice. And that's precisely why Jesus died. So let's do a bit of simple mathematics here and celebrate:

punishment for sin = death
Jesus's death = payment in full
result = no punishment left

It is because of Jesus that God is good to you. And it is because of Jesus's fully satisfying sacrifice that God is good to you *all* the time. So God's not up in heaven swirling around and around in some barbershop chair, with his face toward you when you're good and his back to you when you've blown it. His face is *always* toward you. That's the gospel truth about your fellowship—your permanent connection to God's Spirit.

Embrace God's Grace

So what will be the result of teaching this total forgiveness to people? Many are afraid of what this sort of grace might lead to. They think this unconditional flavor of grace (which is the *only* kind of grace there is, by the way!) will lead to a massive sinfest. Well, God himself seems to think differently about that! Titus 2:12 reveals that God's grace not only brings us salvation, but *God's grace also teaches us to say no to sin and to live upright lives right here and now.*

So don't be afraid of grace. It's time to embrace God's grace to the fullest—to hear about it, believe it to the fullest, and then *relax* in it!

8

You Won't Be Judged for Your Sins

What will Jesus see in me when he returns? Will he be disgusted with me?

Some of us freak out about the return of Christ. We're plagued by questions like these.

"I may just barely squeak into heaven," some think.

This stirs up anxiety, not relaxation.

But can we afford to relax even about the final judgment? The answer to that one is a resounding *yes*. First John 4:17–18 says we can have total confidence in the day of judgment. It says that if we are fearful, it's only because we must be imagining some kind of punishment we'll receive. If we are fearful, then we simply need a bigger dose of God's perfect love.

We're supposed to have total confidence, not fear, about Christ's return. After all, what in the world are we afraid of? That he will refer back to our sins in some way and judge us for them? He already had all of our sins in mind when he treated the entire sin issue on the cross! The punishment was death, and Jesus died. It's all over. So when he comes back, it's not to judge us for our sins or even to refer to our sins in any way. Instead, we are assured that he "will appear a second time for salvation *without reference to sin*, to those who eagerly await Him" (Heb. 9:28 NASB).

The Judgment Seat

But doesn't 2 Corinthians 5:10 say that we must *all* appear before the judgment seat of Christ? Well, yes, there will certainly be "all" of us appearing there—all *humans*. But unbelievers get one destiny and believers get another.

It's not supposed to be stressful for us in the least!

I know what you may have heard—that there are two judgments: a *main* judgment concerning heaven or hell and then a *second* judgment for Christians at the *bēma* (Greek term) or judgment seat of Christ. You may have been taught that this *bēma* seat judgment is a place of *only* rewarding. Some claim that *bēma* is a word that comes from the Greek Olympic games, and therefore it describes a place of positive, rewards-only judgment. From there they reason that the Great White Throne Judgment (from Rev. 20:11–15) and the *bēma* seat judgment are two distinct events, the first being about heaven or hell and the second being for Christians to get varying degrees of heavenly rewards.

But here's the truth. The word *bēma* actually appears about a dozen times in the Bible to describe things like Pilate's judgment seat (Matt. 27:19; John 19:13), Herod Agrippa's throne (Acts 12:21), the Jewish proconsul Gallio's judgment seat (Acts 18:12), and Caesar's judgment seat (Acts 25:10), as well as the judgment seat of Christ (2 Cor. 5:10) and other things too. So a *bēma* is not a sweet, warm place of rewarding. It appears plenty of times in the Bible as a place from which judgment and punishment were doled out.

Given the true meaning of *bēma*, it does *not* appear that a *bēma* seat judgment is a second event, held later, for Christians. At least, there's not any real reason to conclude that, especially when Revelation 21:3–5 already tells us that Christians appear at a judgment and hear from their heavenly Father that there is no death, no mourning, no pain, and that God will be with us forever. So where's the part when God says to a Christian, "Hey, Billy, you did super great on earth. Let me give you some extra loot that nobody else gets"? Well, we don't see that. In fact, in the parable of the vineyard workers, they all lined up to get paid, and no matter how long they'd been working, they all got paid the same (Matt. 20:1–16)!

Ouch. Now that's an assault on the ego. That stings.

You might be thinking, "So, you're telling me that some guy"—we often like to add, "like Hitler!"—"can wait until he's on his deathbed to receive the offer of eternal life and then still receive the same benefit as Billy Graham?" Good question. It seems that the answer is yes. And that's offensive, isn't it? Grace offends human pride. So I guess we either get with the program of receiving free grace, or we live our lives offended at God's new way.

The choice is ours.

There Are No Shoats or Geep!

Here's another way to put it, using the analogy that Jesus gave us in Matthew 25. There are sheep, and then there are goats. But there are no shoats or geep! There is no third animal, no sheep-goat hybrid. So you either get an inheritance as a sheep or you get eternal fire as a goat (Matt. 25:34, 41). But you don't get some sort of "flaming inheritance" with a bit of hell mixed in. It's black and white, all or nothing, with no middle ground!

But maybe we still think we're going to get a huge payoff of heavenly loot when we get there if we've been really good. I don't know where that comes from, because I don't even see the word *rewards* (plural, with an *s*) in the Bible. I do see that there's the "crown of life" for all who love Jesus, but Jesus *is* life to us (Col. 3:4; James 1:12). There's a "reward" (singular), but everything else is dung next to knowing Christ (1 Cor. 3:14; Phil. 3:8). And there's a "prize" mentioned too (Phil. 3:14), but isn't Jesus also our prize?

I know there'll be a great place for us to live. Jesus said he would take care of that (John 14:2–3). I just think we're pretty far off track when we start imagining ourselves on a podium receiving a bunch of gold neck chains. We're pretty far off track when we imagine ourselves in a tricked-out heavenly crib looking over at our neighbor who's living in a cardboard box because he didn't perform as well as we did. The way I read John 14:2–3, there's actually *one big house* (Jesus called it his Father's house), and there are *many rooms* in that heavenly house. It's not really about "my mansion versus your double-wide" anyway.

It's about togetherness as the household of God.

I know what it says in 1 Corinthians 3:15: if what a person builds is burned up, "the builder will suffer loss." But it seems to me that the "loss" is the loss of his work. After all, it was burned up, because it was all human effort! So it was time and energy wasted. That's the loss. Should we expect works of the flesh to be preserved forever? Of course not, so that is the loss—the loss of the work itself. That's very different from God dishing out varying amounts of cash prizes based on our work. That's not grace.

Grace means . . . *everything* is free!

Earth Coming at You. Christ in You.

As I write these words, Oklahoma City and surrounding areas have recently experienced two devastating tornados. Many were killed, including men, women, and children. Illness, death, natural disasters—these things are *not* thrown at us by God. While some popular televangelists may disagree, we need to get the truth firmly implanted in our minds if we're going to *relax* in the finished work of Jesus.

Earth comes *at* us, but Christ works *in* us. God is our comforter and counselor in the midst of trouble. He never promises to remove the trouble, nor is he hurling it at us. Think about what the Son of God himself went through.

70

Was he trouble free? Did he avoid disaster? Jesus was mocked, beaten, pierced, tortured, and killed.

The apostle Paul tells us, "let this mind be in you which was also in Christ Jesus" (Phil. 2:5 NKJV). God's agenda is that we be conformed to his Son's image. This could not happen if we were to somehow magically eject from life's difficult circumstances. So we're not escaping those hard times, but God is *not* causing them either.

Remember: Earth comes *at* you, but Christ works *in* you.

There's another flavor of the gospel out there that says that if you have enough faith, you can find smooth sailing and easy living. This leads people to conversely conclude that if your circumstances are bad, then God must be trying to "teach you a lesson." If you were only more faithful or more obedient, you'd experience relief, they might tell you. Yes, there is a form of relief here and now. But relief comes from within, not from without. *Many times, relief comes not from new circumstances but from new covenant thoughts in the midst of the same old circumstances.*

Look, you simply cannot relax with God if you think he might be the evil author of your painful circumstances. He is not the author of your pain. He is your great Comforter in the midst of it all. He is the author and perfecter of your faith, not your trouble (Heb. 12:2)!

God Wants to Save, Not Kill

On September 11, 2001, terrorists crashed airplanes into buildings on the east coast of the United States. Christian leaders came out in droves to tell us why these things happened. Much like the story of Job and his friends, there's always an "expert" on hand to tell you that God is mad and that humanity's moral failings are the reason.

But 2 Peter 3:9 says that God doesn't want anyone to perish. He wants everyone to believe and be saved. That's what is on his heart for humanity. So he's not really going about the business of killing people. No, it's *saving* people that is on his agenda (John 12:47). It'd make no sense if God were striking whole cities (men, women, and children) with early death when his heart is for them to believe and thereby be saved.

People are always pulling out their favorite war story from Israel's archives to say God is still violently punishing sin today. But that was under the old covenant, *not* the new covenant. Yes, it's the same God, but it's a different covenant.

That makes a huge difference!

Remember that one main point of the new covenant message is that the offer of salvation has now been unleashed on *everyone*, both Jew and Gentile, for the first time ever (Rom. 1:16; 2 Cor. 5:19; 1 John 2:2). So salvation is what God wants for everyone. At least, that is what is on his heart, whether we comply with it or not. To say otherwise is to wrongly label the sinful and harmful work of Satan as coming from God!

But What about Ananias and Sapphira?

But wait, didn't God kill Ananias and Sapphira for lying about money (Acts 5:1–11)? And doesn't that mean, as some say, "God will take Christians out of commission if they don't live for him"?

First, the Scripture never actually says that Ananias and Sapphira were believers. Sure, they were hanging out with the church, but there's simply not any evidence one way or another. Also, it doesn't say that God killed them. We might assume that God struck them dead, but it only says that they fell dead.

At the time, the apostles were likely pretty intimidating as they were powerfully teaching the gospel, healing people, and working miracles. Imagine if you told a lie about money and an apostle discerned the truth and caught you in the lie! In that scenario, I could see somebody being so shocked that they have a heart attack.

Regardless of their cause of death, we still don't know if they were Christians. And, again, we don't know if they were struck dead by God. There's no way to tell. But we do know this: Acts is a descriptive history book recounting the "acts" of the apostles. Acts tells us *what* happened but *not why* it occurred.

Think about this one: In the book of Acts, tongues of fire fell on people's heads. So is that the sign of true salvation? Should we make that into a doctrine for today? If so, then no one today is truly saved. See what I mean? We don't extract doctrine from the events in Acts. It's just like if we were to reach back to the historical account of Jonah and then create a doctrine of "if you disobey God, you may be swallowed by a whale!" Sure, that was a historical occurrence, but it's not something we mold into a doctrine for today.

The story in Acts about Ananias and Sapphira should not be spun into a modern-day belief of "God's gonna getcha!" God is not killing Christians for lies they tell. After all, if God were killing Christians for lying about money, our Sunday services would be littered with corpses!

Remember that the whole point of the gospel is that Jesus was killed in our place for the lies we tell. So when it comes to judgment and punishment, you really can . . . *relax.*

PART 2

RELAX IN THE REALITY OF THE RESURRECTION

9

You Don't Need to Kill Yourself

You may have heard someone say, "As a Christian, I need to die to self. It needs to be all of God and none of me. I must decrease so that he can increase."

Many of us seem to be infatuated with killing ourselves, diminishing ourselves, or somehow preventing ourselves from being an obstacle to God. We are getting in God's way, we think. We suspect that we are the problem. We are not compatible with Jesus and what he wants to do with us. So maybe he is looking to remove us from the equation or get rid of some ugly part of us, we might think.

"Yeah, I know my old sinner self got put on the altar, but I guess I keep trying to crawl off!" We get a bit of questionable theology in the mix, and the picture isn't any clearer. It's pretty hard to relax with God if we think that we are just a tiny bit detestable to him as we currently are.

What's missing? We're neglecting a basic message of Christianity—that we *already* died with Christ (Rom. 6:6; Gal. 2:20). So we try to die again or die more. But our old self already died with him, not on an altar but on a cross. And that death was final (Rom. 6:10–11). We died to sin. We died to the law (Gal. 2:19). But we didn't just die; we were resurrected and made new at the core (Rom. 6:4; Eph. 2:6). So why are we trying to kill what has already been made new?

It's so human to try to better ourselves or to want to clean ourselves and then somehow hit a "restart" button each and every day. We think we are the problem, when, counterintuitively, *we are actually now part of the solution.* God doesn't want to replace us—he already did with a new self, a new creation. We are now his spiritual offspring (John 3:6; Rom. 6:13; 1 Cor. 6:17). So he doesn't want to replace us. He wants to embrace us!

The Art of Doing Nothing

We want to be "like Jesus," and so we try to behave like him. We might hope that little by little, our nature will change more every day. But the truth is that deep down at our core, we *are* like him: "In this world we are like Jesus" (1 John 4:17).

There's a big difference between wanting to be like Jesus and realizing that because of a radical, spiritual heart surgery, you *are* like Jesus! One view incites effort. The other relaxation, spiritual rest. So what if we really are like him? What if we have his Spirit (Rom. 5:5; Titus 3:5–6), his nature (2 Pet. 1:4), and his mind (1 Cor. 2:16) within us? And what if he changed us—our spirit and our heart—so that we now "fit" with him (Ezek. 36:26–27; 1 Cor. 6:17)?

After all, who told you there was something wrong with you? God asked Adam in the Garden long ago, "Who told you that you were naked?" (Gen. 3:11), and thousands of years later, we're still cowering in the corner, ashamed, covering ourselves with leaves of self-improvement.

We might even think it's humble to go there, to act dirty and distant. But it's not humility. It may actually be pride, a "victim flavor" of self-focus: "Look at me. Look how lowly and sinful I am. I'm not worthy! I'm not worthy!"

The true gospel message frees us to get our eyes off of false humility and put them on Jesus. In fact, God has rigged it so that we can do exactly that! Your forgiveness means you can forget about your past. Your acceptance means you can forget about if you're "good enough." Your closeness to God means you can forget about trying to get close, because you're already as close to God as you'll ever be (Rom. 6:5; 1 Cor. 6:17).

Get off that train.

Stop trying to get close. Stop trying to stay close. Relax. Practice the art of doing nothing—nothing to achieve *more* forgiveness, nothing to achieve *more* acceptance, and nothing to achieve *more* closeness. There's simply nothing you *can* do to become "more dead" and then "more alive" in Christ. Spiritually, we were crucified on that cross. Christ's death was "once for all," and our death to sin was likewise "once for all" (Rom. 6:10–11).

So die to self? Rid yourself of your self?

Little by little, die to sin more?

Spiritual death with Christ is not progressive. Our death to sin doesn't take place through Bible study or prayer or church attendance. It *only* happens through crucifixion. You can't crucify yourself either. (Picture that one: You nail one hand up. Where do you go from there?) No, crucifixion has to happen *to* you. And, fortunately, it has! So simply rest in that reality. It's over. All you really can do is realize it, set your mind on who you are now, and relax. "Count yourselves dead to sin but alive to God in Christ Jesus" (Rom. 6:11).

Monty Python Theology

I know, I know. You've been fed that bit about needing to "die daily." But that's all a misunderstanding. Paul says that *one* time, but he's talking about being attacked by wild dogs while he is out on a country road (1 Cor. 15:30–32). Paul literally meant that he faced death daily—physical death. He never intended us to take that verse and twist it into some sort of dark, cruel spiritual death that needs to keep happening daily, over and over. It's not a *Monty Python and the Holy Grail* theology of being "mostly dead."

But aren't we supposed to take up our cross? Doesn't Jesus tell us to do that (Matt. 16:24)?

Yes, but when Jesus took up his cross, where did he go? To Calvary. So if we take up our cross and follow him, where would we end up? At Calvary with him, to die. And that's precisely what happened to us when we believed—we were crucified with him (Rom. 6:6; Gal. 2:20)!

Yeah, but what about when he says to take up your cross *daily* (Luke 9:23)?

There's no question that we're supposed to wake up daily and count ourselves dead to sin and alive to God (Rom. 6:11), but that's very different from trying to kill ourselves off again. What God is telling us is to daily consider ourselves as being new in Jesus Christ, because we *are* new. There's no room for a "split personality Christianity" in which we're half-old and half-new and we're trying to suppress (or murder) half of us! That's a bit like Eastern religion, not Christianity.

Hardware vs. Software

You might be thinking, "Sounds nice, but I still sin. All the time! So this sounds like it's a 'name it and claim it' thing to me. Let's be real!"

Yeah, I know you still sin. I do too! But this is not some name it and claim it approach. What I'm saying is: it doesn't matter if you name it or claim it. If you are in Christ, it's true. You *are* new. And here's the thing: you're going to prove your new identity one way or another—either by sinning and being miserable (because you're not made for it!) or by living in dependency on Christ and being fulfilled. Either way, you prove that you are a peculiar person, out of the ordinary—a new creation that is like Jesus at the core (2 Cor. 5:17; 1 John 4:17). You're not like the guy next door.

Yes, we're still learning and growing in our knowledge of Jesus (2 Pet. 3:18). There's change going on in our minds, as our mindsets are experiencing a complete overhaul. But that doesn't mean that our spiritual death with Christ was bogus. It definitely happened. But it was a spiritual surgery, not a mental one. At the center of your spiritual being, it happened. But much like a mobile device is constantly being offered a new download, our minds are being offered "updates" of truth: "be transformed by the renewing of your mind" (Rom. 12:2). Still, even with those software downloads still happening, remember that the spiritual *hardware* itself (our human spirit) is brand new and de-signed to operate with the latest soul software!

Don't mistake the software for the hardware. Yeah, loads of Christians these days think they have a "sinful nature" and maybe another (new) nature right beside it. You know, two natures. This misconception comes about because *we still sin and need to explain why.* In so doing, we might mistake the software (which is in need of updates) for the hardware. We might think that because we've still got loads of stinking thinking to deal with, our hearts must still be sinful and wicked.

Sinful Nature or Flesh?

An error in a popular translation—the New International Version (NIV 1984)—hasn't helped the issue much either. Christians are trying to sort out how they can be new spiri-tual creations in Christ (dead to sin and alive to God) and yet still get those embarrassing, sinful thoughts in their minds. Meanwhile, the NIV was communicating that they have a "sinful nature." But "sinful nature" is not even a remotely good translation of the Greek word *sarx* used in Galatians 5 and Romans 7–8, among other places.

The Greek term *sarx* simply means "flesh." It's not our spiritual nature. No, our spiritual nature is new, not sinful. Remember that our old self was crucified with Christ, and we did indeed become new creations at our spiritual core (Rom. 6:6; 2 Cor. 5:17).

To their credit, after thirty years, the publishers of the NIV fixed the error in a new edition. And now we're all playing catch-up. But what was the collateral damage of the "sinful nature" translation? Believers have been running around thinking that their spiritual nature is still dirty and ugly, or at least half of it is. We say we are desperately wicked, and we think we are humble to hold that view.

But you tell me: if God intervenes in our lives, kills our old self, resurrects us and re-creates us for good works with a new spirit, a new heart, and God's Spirit permanently sealed within us, then what's your best guess about our spiritual nature? The fact is that we are so new and different now that we even get to "participate in the divine nature" (2 Pet. 1:4)!

If we want to understand what *sarx* ("the flesh") actually is, then it's best to go right to the source—the Bible—to see how the word is used there. And this is what we find:

1. The flesh is something we set our mind on (Rom. 8:6–7 NASB).
2. The flesh is something we walk according to (2 Cor. 10:3; Gal. 5:16).
3. The flesh battles against the Spirit (Gal. 5:17).
4. The flesh is equivalent to the way of human effort (Gal. 3:3).

5. The flesh builds strength and status—a résumé (1 Cor. 1:26; Phil. 3:4–6).

6. The flesh can become the object of our confidence (Phil. 3:4).

The flesh is not your spiritual nature. In other words, the flesh is *not your old self* coming back to life somehow. No, your old self was crucified, buried, and is now gone. The flesh is simply "residue" left over within your thinking and approaches to life. After all, when you became a believer, did you wake up the next morning with all new thinking in every way? Of course not! But you did wake up with that new spirit, that new heart, and those new desires in your innermost being.

So what is the flesh exactly? The flesh is a way to think or act. The flesh is a network of habits and strategies that we employ to make it through life, avoid pain, and seek success. Going back to the computer analogy, the flesh is like out-of-date software running in our soul (mind, will, emotions) that is incompatible with our new spiritual hardware (our new human spirit). The flesh is the mental realm (network of thoughts) that we live from when we ignore our union with Christ. It's a worldly approach to life that we can set our mind on or put confidence in.

But the flesh is *not* us! This is why, as believers, when we set our minds on the worldly way of thinking (the flesh), it just never pays off. It can look good to us. It can even take on a well-adjusted, self-improving appearance. Or it might take on an ugly do-whatever-it-takes-to-please-myself-and-get-ahead look. But both are messed-up ways of thinking that will fail us every time.

If we try to make life work via the flesh, it's empty, and it never really pans out. There's no way it can, since God has the market cornered on fulfillment. We can only expect disappointment, confusion, or misery from the flesh.

It's a dead-end street.

Still, based on some of what we hear these days about the Christian life, we might think we should get out there and do our best, and be radical, and change the world! But this only excites religious flesh. Rule-based or self-improving flesh is no better than any other kind of flesh (Gal. 3:3; Col. 2:20–23). When we go that route, we're not trusting in the "growth which is from God" (Col. 2:19 NASB).

So it's important to realize that the "try harder" religious flesh *and* the "give up and live like the devil" flavor of flesh are *both* off base. There is a third way, a better way—relaxing in the sufficiency of God's Spirit (2 Cor. 12:9; Gal. 5:16).

10

You're New on the Inside

The flesh doesn't work alone. The flesh has an ally, a collaborator called *sin*. Here we're talking about sin as a noun. You know, a person, place, thing, or idea. Not a verb (like *sinning*), but a noun—a thing. And if you were to consult a dictionary of New Testament words, you'd learn that this noun *sin* is person-like in its characteristics. It strategizes, tempts, and *acts through the body* when it can.

This means a sin parasite feeds us thoughts.

This is huge. We can finally explain what is going on in our thought lives. We're not dirty. We're not ugly. But sin is! This power called sin has access to us, but it's *not* us (Rom. 7:17, 20). It's a rogue agent acting through us, when we let it (Rom. 6:12).

Realizing the real source of temptation can make all the difference!

The Temptation-Accusation Cycle

The percentage of men who have gotten into pornography is pretty high. A quick review of all the surveys out there reveals that somewhere between 50 and 80 percent of men look at porn. Fortunately, the stats for Christian men are *way* different at around 50 to 80 percent. (Note: that's not a typo, but it *is* a bit of sarcasm.)

At least once a month I get an email from someone who wants help getting out of a porn addiction. Some men feel "stuck" in it, like they can't stop. Then, on top of that, they feel super alone in guilt and shame when no one else they know struggles with it—or at least no one admits to it! The power of sin is offering men first the *temptation* and then the *accusation* once they give in.

They first feel controlled, then blamed and shamed.

The percentage of women who look at pornography is lower but still in the 20 to 40 percent range. Christian women report that in addition to fantasy and lust, some of their main struggles include bitterness, resentment, criticism or slander, and lack of trust. First they feel controlled by this sort of thinking. Then they feel guilty for being controlled by it! Again, the power of sin offers them *tempting* thoughts, and then it *accuses* them of generating those thoughts. They too feel controlled, then blamed and shamed as they entertain thoughts like, "If I were a real Christian, I wouldn't think these things!"

No matter your struggle, you are all too familiar with this cycle. You've lived it. But what if you need to rethink what is happening to you in those moments? What if you are not the source of the thoughts that plague you? *Are you willing to consider reinterpreting your whole thought life in a brand-new way?*

You Are *Not* What You Think!

You know, the Bible says that we are new creations (2 Cor. 5:17), we have the mind of Christ (1 Cor. 2:16), we are God's workmanship (Eph. 2:10), and we are spiritually seated with Christ right next to God (Eph. 2:6). So what if there's nothing actually wrong with who you are?

We might imagine that God somehow flubbed it up when he got to us in particular. So let me ask you: What if he didn't flub it up? What if the whole reason you've doubted your cleanness and your closeness to God is because of the thoughts that swirl around in your head? And what if those thoughts aren't even originating with you to begin with? What if you truly are who God says you are? After all, when our view of ourselves disagrees with *God's* view of us, who's right?

I have seen the truths of our new identity in Christ save marriages and restore shattered lives. I've seen husbands and wives unite together as a team, no longer looking at their spouse as the enemy, but instead together labeling sin as their common enemy. Once they shifted the blame toward the deceiving parasite called sin, they could begin to look at the porn struggle or the bitterness issue or whatever it might be from a whole new perspective. They realized that they weren't actually fighting each other; the battle was "not against flesh and blood" (Eph. 6:12) but instead against a third-party deceiver called sin. With this in mind, they not only began to recognize their true enemy but also began to more fully realize *each other's* identity in Christ. They could see more clearly the new, trustworthy heart that God had given their spouse. Through these powerful truths, the road to restoration was opened.

We have two options: we can live in the beautiful reality of who we really are, or we can live in a debilitating delusion. So what if you truly were crucified with Christ, buried with Christ, and raised with Christ? What if you really went through a spiritual surgery that left you new at the core? What if you don't really want to sin? What if every time you do end up sinning, you're actually going *against* your nature?

You Are Not a Pink Flamingo!

Maybe you've heard the popular idea that you might not fully belong to God quite yet. Some Bible teachers say you're like a house with many rooms, and when you "gave your life to Christ," maybe you didn't give all of yourself to him. They say perhaps there are more rooms you need to open to him so he can come in and clean house, taking more and more ownership of you.

Now, I see where these guys are coming from, but allow me to take their analogy and play with it a bit. Look, you are a person of God's own possession (Eph. 1:14). God cleaned house (forgiveness), and then he moved in (by his Spirit). You are 100 percent God's, and he doesn't share you with anyone or anything else. So you don't need to worry about how much of you is new or clean or owned by God. All of you—body, soul, and spirit—is fully and completely his (1 Cor. 6:19–20).

But we do have some pink flamingos in the yard that have got to go! Heck, there's even an engine hanging from that tree over there! And the neighbors have taken notice of our redneck ways. So yeah, our house is indeed clean, and God has fully moved in. But outwardly, when it comes to the attitudes and actions we put on display in the yard, there's still some work to be done. And that is where our growth comes into play.

Still, while there's progress to be made in terms of what the neighbors see on the outside, you need not worry about how much of your house is actually owned by the Lord. Rest assured—you are not a pink flamingo! You are not what you do. You are a child of God, and you *fully* belong to Jesus Christ.

A Righteousness That Matters

Another popular thing we're hearing these days is the idea that we Christians are not really righteous. We're just seen by God *as if* we are righteous, some say, in a "positional" sense.

This sort of teaching says we don't have any real righteousness here and now on planet Earth. Instead, God is up in heaven essentially pretending we are righteous. He's looking at us through a special lens, maybe some "Jesus glasses." Or even more likely, he's looking at Jesus *instead* of us! He can't stand to look our way, because we're too hideously sinful. So he looks away to Jesus instead, essentially to grin and bear our existence.

Have you heard this idea? It sounds right at first, but the logic breaks down anytime you hit one of those "new creation" passages—you know, the ones about us being a new self, or a new creation, or born again, or born of the Spirit, or born of God (John 3:6–7; 1 Pet. 1:3; 1 John 3:9). Apparently, according to those passages, God *birthed* us spiritually, so we are *actually* new and different at the center of our being—in our human spirit.

That's *real* righteousness! When the core of your being has been ripped out and terminated and then replaced with a new core, then something dramatic has happened. And that something means that you are righteous now. It's not a pretend righteousness but a real righteousness—the kind that brings power for change right here on planet Earth, not later when we supposedly swallow a yellow righteousness pill right before we hit the pearly gates.

Think about it. The Bible does say we get new resurrection bodies in the future (Rom. 8:23; 2 Cor. 5:2), but that's it! There's no mention of any last-minute polish of us spiritually, because in our spirits, we've *already* been changed. We've become "the righteousness of God" (2 Cor. 5:21).

We are heaven-ready on the inside!

But some preachers go around saying that we Christians have a sinful, wicked heart. Well, if that's true, then what in the world does it mean to have a *new* heart and a *new* spirit, and God's Spirit living in us? I mean, did God actually change us in a tangible way or not?

How can we get this wrong? How can so many preachers who read the same Bible miss this one? The answer is pretty straightforward, I think. They're supposing that we received some "thing" called salvation (like an entrance ticket) and some new "place" to go called heaven, and that's about it.

But there's so much more!

You were changed. You got a DNA swap, an identity switch. Your heart isn't sinful anymore; it's new (Ezek. 36:26; Rom. 6:17)! Do you not sense your heart tugging at you to believe this is the truth—that, even now in this world, you are like Jesus in your innermost being (1 John 4:17)?

Simul justus et peccator?

We hear some folks saying, "Yeah, but Paul called himself 'chief of sinners' (see 1 Tim. 1:15), so this can't be right. We are both sinners and saints by nature, at the same time!" Then they throw out the Latin phrase *Simul justus et peccator* (translation: "Simultaneously saint and sinner") made popular long ago, so it all sounds scholarly and official.

So it must be true, right? Wrong.

First, I say to that: *Desine duplicem sermonem* (translation: "Stop the double-talk!"). We are not simultaneously saint and sinner by nature! If you look more closely at what Paul was saying, it's clear that he was talking about his former life as a killer of Christians (1 Tim. 1:13–16). As a Pharisee and persecutor of the church, in his mind he set a world record for heinous sins *in his past* and in this sense arrived at being a "chief of sinners." But then God saved him and changed him into a new, righteous saint!

That's the point—that no matter what our former identity might have looked like, we now have a new identity—holy, blameless, righteous saint. We shouldn't try to marry our old identity to our new one. It's certainly not spiritual or "scholarly" to do so!

So let's skip the Latin verbiage and simply relax in the reality that Paul addressed the church as saints (not sinners) in nearly every epistle he wrote! We truly are different on the inside, and that's why it's hard for us to go on sinning. In Romans 6:2, Paul asks us: How *can* we live in sin any longer? And 1 John 3:9 says that God's seed remains in us and that we *cannot* go on practicing sin as a consistent lifestyle. We don't want to practice sin to get better at it. We hate it. We abhor it. Yes, we *were* sinners by nature before our new spiritual birth took place. We *were* suckers for sin. But now we have an obedient heart, not a sinful one (Rom. 6:17)!

When temptation strikes, the enemy wants to put us in a place of panic: *How can I be thinking this? What's wrong with me? If I'm this dirty, I might as well give in!* But what God wants us to do, rather than panic in the moment of temptation, is to *relax* in the reality of our new identity. So let me ask you something:

Do you know who you *really* are?

11

You've Got Resurrection Life

People often talk about eternal life like it's some *thing*, like it's a coupon for heaven or a gift package when we get there. Or we might think of eternal life as a life that is far off, in the future, to be lived later. For us right now, eternal life might be seen as something that we read about in a book or talk about in a building that we sit in for an hour a week.

But eternal life isn't your life made better.

And eternal life isn't your life made longer.

Eternal life is *Christ's* life.

So when we receive eternal life, we actually receive a Person, his life. In John 14:19, Jesus says that we will live forever because he lives forever. Colossians 3:4 tells us that Christ *is* our life. If we were to lose eternal life, it would mean we'd lose Jesus. If we lost Jesus, we'd lose eternal life. They are one and the same. Eternal life is Jesus (1 John 5:12). And it's *his life* (not merely his death) that saves us (Rom. 5:10).

To have Christ is to have salvation. Some people try to push the idea that you can have salvation but not yet have the Spirit. But these are one and the same. To have the Spirit is to have salvation. To have salvation is to have the Spirit. The Spirit of Christ is the Spirit of life (eternal life; Rom. 8:2). You can't have one without the other. Romans 8:9 reveals that if we don't have the Spirit, then we don't belong to God at all. So how much clearer can it be?

You can relax in knowing that you have all of Jesus that you'll ever need, right from the start. You don't need to go shopping for more of Jesus. And when someone comes knocking, telling you that you need this spiritual gift (to be like them), or that second blessing, or an extra dosage of the Spirit, remember that you already have everything you need for life and godliness. You are complete, and you don't lack anything (Col. 2:9–10; 2 Pet. 1:3).

Many today actually glorify the search for more. They tell us that we need to "hunger" for more of God. They tell us that we should "thirst" for more of Jesus. All the while, the Son of God announces the polar opposite: "He who comes to me will never go hungry, and he who believes in me will never be thirsty" (John 6:35).

So rest in what you have. You have all the Jesus you'll ever need (2 Pet. 1:3). And he is enough!

Christ the Vine

It's not about *what* we are doing. It's really about *how* we are doing it. That's all that matters to God (Gal. 5:6; Heb. 11:6). He wants us to bear fruit, but only by faith in our union with Christ. Romans 7:4 tells us that *we died to the law* and were joined (married) to the risen Christ *in order to bear fruit for God.*

Notice the divine order: we died to the law in order to bear fruit. Fruit cannot come from the law. We died to the way of rules and effort so that we can live in this new way—living *from* Jesus (Col. 2:20–23). It's the only way to bear any real fruit at all. The source is everything.

You'll never go into a vineyard and see grapes exerting their best efforts to grow. No, it's about being attached to the vine. That's *all* it's about. Without that connection, there's nothing. So maybe it's time we simply relax into Jesus.

But don't read passivity into that! I simply mean that no amount of human effort accomplishes anything in God's eyes. He wants us to be *receivers* and thereby *transmitters* of his life (John 15:5; Rom. 8:11). So why not just do that very thing? Why not resolve to change the way that we go about living altogether?

Why not live by faith in Christ the Vine, since you are already attached to him? After all, it's your destiny!

All of *You* Too!

Now, remember in all of this that you are compatible with Jesus. Don't fall for the lie that it's just some Sunday school version of you that God loves. No, we're not talking about some kind of faraway "Bible view" of you. The real you, right here and now, fits perfectly with Jesus. Your personality is ready to go, and your body can be his instrument too (as a *living* sacrifice, not a dead one; Rom. 12:1). All of you, every ounce of you, is acceptable to God (Rom. 15:7). That's why we can offer ourselves to him (Rom. 6:13). When we get this truth in our minds, we begin to see that Christ joined to our unique personality is enough for everything that planet Earth might throw our way. So go ahead and say it:

Christ joined to _____ (your name) *is enough!*

So it's *not* "all of him and none of you." You are not some hollow, lifeless tube that he wants to flow through. That would take us toward an Eastern mysticism of sorts. No, this is very different. Instead of all of him and none of you, it's *all* of him and *all* of you in a beautiful spiritual union together (Rom. 6:5; 1 Cor. 6:17).

It's about knowing who you are and then just being yourself. It's about him in you *and* you in him (John 14:20; 15:4; 17:23). It's a partnership. No, you don't supply the spiritual strength. He supplies the strength. But you are the new self, raised and seated with him (Eph. 2:6) and compatible with his heart and his ways. You fit. You fit perfectly with his Spirit and his agenda.

That's a beautiful, relaxing, and equipping message to embrace!

The Truth about Abiding

You may be thinking, "But I so want to *abide*. How do I abide in Christ?"

Yeah, I hear what you're saying. But leave it to us Christians to turn something as beautiful as abiding in Christ into a "work" of abiding that we somehow initiate and sustain! The term *abide* simply means "to live." If you make your abode somewhere, you live there. So to abide in Christ is to live in Christ. Yes, it's that simple—if you are in Christ, then you already abide (live) in Christ.

In fact, Jesus says that anyone who does not abide (live) in Christ is like a branch that is thrown into a fire and burned (John 15:6). Christians aren't going to burn, because we *do* abide in Christ. So rather than making this into some "work" we maintain, what if we instead wake up every day celebrating the awesome reality that we *do* live (abide) in Christ and he lives in us?

Don't get me wrong. Of course, we have moment-by-moment choices to make as we walk around planet Earth and are confronted with temptation. But instead of "trying" to abide (live) in Christ, the truth is that we can now make choices to walk by the Spirit *because we already live in the Spirit*.

Big difference, huh? Our connection with Christ is never lost. He will always live in us, and we will always live in him, no matter our behavior (2 Tim. 2:13; Heb. 7:25; 13:5). But when we walk by him, we are living out our true identity and our God-given destiny. When we don't, and we walk by the flesh, we're settling for a lie and will only find frustration and lack of fulfillment (Gal. 5:16).

So wake up every day, be reminded of who you really are in Christ, and then just be yourself! In so doing, you are both living *in* and walking *by* the Spirit.

Being "Filled with the Spirit"

Another concern might be, "Yeah, but I still want to be filled with the Spirit! How do I know I'm filled? What does it *feel* like?"

Being filled with the Spirit is a concept that has received more than its share of attention. Although this phrase only appears in Acts (with no "how-to" provided) and in Ephesians, it has become the object of much controversy (Acts 2:4; 4:8; 13:52; Eph. 5:18).

While some claim that being filled with the Spirit is synonymous with speaking in tongues, others say that experiences of holy laughter, angelic prayer language, or slayings (falling over in church, hopefully into the arms of someone with the gift of "catching") must be evidenced if one is truly "filled with the Spirit."

There may be as many beliefs about being filled with the Spirit as there are denominations of Christianity! Given the plethora of viewpoints, how is one to know the truth?

As always, the best approach is to consult the Scriptures in context and read God's thoughts on the matter. As I mentioned, there are several instances of people being filled with the Spirit in the book of Acts. But the problem with attempting to extract "how-to" doctrine from these verses is that they're historical accounts, nothing more. They describe the apostles and others as being filled with the Spirit, but they don't teach the reader how to be filled.

In actuality, there's only one epistle in the New Testament—Ephesians—that urges us to be "filled with the Spirit" (5:18). Not surprisingly, the clearest explanation of what it means to be filled with the Spirit is found in that same letter, only two chapters earlier: "to grasp how wide and long and high and deep is the love of Christ, and *to know this love* that surpasses knowledge—*that you may be filled* to the measure of all the fullness of God" (3:18–19). Here Paul says that being filled to the fullness of God is about knowing God's love.

Later, Paul tells the Ephesians not to be drunk with wine but to be filled with God's Spirit instead (5:18). What does wine do? It relaxes you. What does God's unconditional love do? It relaxes you! So when Paul tells the Ephesians to be filled with the Spirit, he's urging them to abandon dependency on a substance to bring them peace and instead to depend on God's incredibly deep love for them (3:14–19).

Grasping God's great love for us is an ongoing adventure, so we find Paul using language in the original Greek that conveys a *lifelong* discovery. Essentially, he says, "be 'being filled' [continually] with the Spirit" (5:18). It's not a one-time event; it's a lifelong relationship with a Person whose love will continue to captivate us!

Being filled with the Spirit is certainly not something for an elite few. Being filled with the Spirit is God's intention for every believer as they discover the depths of his love for them. Being filled with the Spirit isn't about fanaticism, radical experiences, or the display of visible power. Indeed, Paul does talk about power in Ephesians, and he even prays that the Ephesian Christians would have power, but it is *power to grasp the greatness of God's love* (3:17–18).

By the way, I'm not negating that God did some spectacular things among those in Scripture who were "filled with the Spirit," and he still does today! I'm simply pointing out what "filled with the Spirit" means from Paul's viewpoint in Ephesians, which is the only epistle that tells us to be filled. Sure, various people in Acts spoke and acted *while inspired by the love of God.* But the events themselves were not what "being filled" was about. Apparently, from God's perspective, being "filled with the Spirit" (knowing his love) is needed even to wait on tables: "Brothers and sisters, choose seven men from among you who are known to be full of the Spirit and wisdom. We will turn this responsibility [serving food] over to them" (Acts 6:3).

The enemy has convinced many believers that being filled with the Spirit is not for them, either because it's too mystical and weird or because it seems too difficult to achieve. But when we consult the Scriptures, we find that being filled with the Spirit is all about *knowing God's love.* We learn that it's a lifelong adventure and that it's compatible with the makeup of every child of God. After all, which of us doesn't want to grasp God's love for us? So when it comes to being filled with the Spirit, you can just *relax* and get to know your Father's great love for you!

12

You Can't Lose Your Salvation

Hebrews 6 and 10 have become weapons of choice for those who argue that we can lose our salvation. Hebrews 6:6 talks about those who have "fallen away," and Hebrews 10:26 speaks of there being "no sacrifice" left for those who deliberately keep on sinning. Some latch on to these phrases and thereby conclude that we Christians can fall away and somehow exhaust the blood of Jesus.

But remember that Hebrews was written to . . . *Hebrews*! Profound, huh? And chapter 5 reveals that many of these Jewish readers needed the "milk" of the gospel all over again (v. 12). They were simply not getting it. Yeah, they were flirting with the gospel message, but at the same time they were going back to the Jewish temple for answers. They were riding on the fence about the whole Jesus thing, so some needed to repent from the dead temple works and stop hedging their bets (Heb. 6:1–2).

This is why the author of Hebrews issues a warning in chapter 6 about subjecting Jesus to public disgrace (v. 6). How could they possibly subject him to *public* disgrace? By publicly trotting back to the temple to seek forgiveness when they'd already heard about the blood of Christ!

See, the people getting this letter (or at least some of them) had shared in all that the Holy Spirit was doing in Jerusalem through the apostles—miracles, healings, even people rising from the dead! They had tasted all of these things, and they had the best gospel teachers on the planet right there in their hometown—the apostles themselves!

What more could you ask for?

Still, these people were *tasting* the gospel but not swallowing it to the point where it fed them (Heb. 6:4–5). It's like when you go down the grocery store aisle and a worker gives you one of those samples. You reach out, grab the toothpick, and ease that little taste-tester portion right into your mouth. But then you say, "No thanks," and walk away. You were willing to try just a bit, but you're not investing in the meal.

The problem is that not investing in Jesus means you've got no other real option out there. You're saying the crucifixion is not good enough for you. You're saying God needs to do more for you than he already did through Jesus. In essence, you're "crucifying the Son of God all over again" (Heb. 6:6) as you insult his finished work! So if you reject him, there's no hope for any salvation outside of him.

That's what Hebrews 6 is really talking about. That's why the writer gives us the analogy of ground that "drinks in" the rain versus ground that doesn't (v. 7). This is much like the parable in Matthew 13:1–8 about various soils, some of which received the seed and some that didn't. Likewise, Hebrews 6 is talking about receiving or rejecting the gospel, not about first being saved and then later losing your salvation.

That's also why the writer concludes his big warning with a clarification: "But, beloved, *we are convinced of better things concerning you*, and things that accompany salvation, though we are speaking in this way" (v. 9 NASB). He's basically saying, "I know what I just finished saying sounds scary, but hey, Christians, I'm not talking about you. As far as you are concerned, there's a much better message for you, a message of great things that accompany your salvation, even though I'm speaking in this way to those who are still riding on the fence."

What about Hebrews 10?

Hebrews 10 is the other biggie when it comes to the claim that we can lose our salvation. This passage alone has caused many Christians to quiver in their boots. It says: "If we deliberately *keep on sinning* after we have received the knowledge of the truth, *no sacrifice for sins is left*, but only a fearful expectation of *judgment* and of *raging fire* that will consume the enemies of God" (vv. 26–27).

Does too much sinning mean we lose our salvation? Gosh, that would mean that most of us . . . well, c'mon, that would mean that *all* of us would be in serious trouble! After all, even the apostle James admits that "we all stumble in many ways" (3:2). So can a certain amount of sinning be too much for God to forgive? Does God suddenly throw away the concept of forgiving people "seventy times seven" times (that's 490 times! See Matt. 18:21–22) when it comes to his own forgiveness of us? And how would we know (without an incredible memory and a smartphone app!) when we've reached the threshold and should now expect the judgment and the fire?

Fortunately, the meaning of this Hebrews 10 passage is straightforward, and it has nothing to do with Christians exhausting the grace of God. The reality is that there is only *one* type of sinning mentioned in the book of Hebrews from chapter 1 all the way up to chapter 10. That's right—just one type of sin, the sin of *unbelief* (Heb. 3:18–19). So what the writer means here, in context, is that if we *keep on unbelieving* even "after we have received the knowledge of the truth" (Heb. 10:26), then there is no adequate sacrifice found anywhere else—especially not in the Jewish temple!

In other words, if any one of us takes a pass on Jesus, then there is only judgment and fire for the "enemies of God" (v. 27). Notice that word *enemies*. This whole thing is directed at unbelievers who oppose God as they keep on rejecting the most amazing message on the planet. So of course, there's no sacrifice left for them! Whose sacrifice would it be? They've already rejected Jesus's sacrifice. And the blood of bulls and goats is no answer at all.

This is very different from scaring Christians to death with the idea that maybe, just maybe, they are struggling too much with sin, so God is going to give them the axe. It's like we're equating God with Santa, only in the worst way ever: "You better watch out . . . God is coming to town! . . . He's gonna find out who's naughty and nice . . . He knows if you've been bad or good . . . Oh, you better watch out!"

The blood of Christ is not going to run out on you. The real point here is that there is no *other* sacrifice outside of Christ. It's Jesus or nothing at all. So whatever you do, don't reject the gospel!

I realize there's that bit in verse 29 about a "sanctified" person who's disrespecting Jesus and what he "deserves." That verse can make Christians think the whole chapter is about them. But consider the whole verse—*it's a hypothetical and rhetorical question addressed to us, the readers.* The writer is asking us as readers to decide, based on the punishment that Jews got when they rejected the law, what *we think* a person should *deserve* (but not necessarily *get*) if they insult God's Spirit.

Of course, true Christians are forgiven and not punished for our many sins and insults to God. But we'd all certainly agree that we do *deserve* death, even though we don't get that punishment. And that's the point here. Whether you're lost or saved (sanctified), the blood of Jesus deserves your full respect, so don't flirt with Jewish religion or any other means of forgiveness and cleansing.

Jesus is all you need, and he deserves to be honored.

Now, the author of Hebrews knows that he has likely freaked everyone out with his words. So he finishes his thoughts in this chapter with the following: "But *we do not belong to those who shrink back* and are destroyed, but to those who have faith and are saved" (v. 39). So Christians are not the ones who were shrinking back from the gospel message. Christians are saved. But those who heard the gospel and then rejected it due to Jewish peer pressure, well, that was a totally different story!

Relax: God's Grace Won't Run Out on You!

If grace is extended to us only on the condition that we behave, then how much sin is too much? When is the grace exhausted? Where is the line? Have you or I exhausted the blood of Christ? How would we even know?

Yes, the Bible speaks of God motivating us to live uprightly, to display self-control, and to say no to sin. Yes, God is relentless in his tutelage of us. But obeying him is not what keeps us saved any more than obeying him is what got us saved in the first place!

No, it was the grace of God that saved us, and it is the grace of God that sustains us. Perhaps Hebrews puts it best: "Therefore he is able to save *completely* those who come to God through him, *because he always lives* to intercede for them" (7:25). Apparently, we are saved *completely*, and our salvation is secured by the length of Jesus's (eternal) life.

We will be saved as long as Jesus lives!

13

You Have the Faith
and the Works

Another weapon in the lose-your-salvation arsenal seems to be the "continue" verses. You know, the verses that seem to say "if you continue," everything will be fine. But they also can sound like they're saying, "Hey, Christian, if you *don't* do your part to continue, then you're going to lose your salvation."

Here's one of the best examples:

> But now he has reconciled you by Christ's physical body through death to present you holy in his sight, without blemish and free from accusation—*if you continue* in your faith, established and firm, and do not move from the hope held out in the gospel. This is the gospel that *you heard* and that *has been proclaimed* to every creature under heaven, and of which I, Paul, have become a servant. (Col. 1:22–23)

First, keep in mind that "continuing" (in obedient behavior) was an *old* covenant problem: "They did not *remain faithful* to my covenant, and I turned away from them, declares the Lord" (Heb. 8:9). And that old covenant problem was solved in the *new* covenant. Remember, that is precisely why God swore by himself, making an oath that serves as our "anchor for the soul" (Heb. 6:19). We are both saved and preserved because of this promise that God made to God, not because we do our part to "continue" for the rest of our lives.

So here's what's actually happening with the "continue" verses. Back in the days of the early church, there were no Billy Graham salvation prayers. There were no altar calls (and there shouldn't be any altar calls today, by the way, as the cross replaced all the altars!). Simply put, there was only hearing with faith (Gal. 3:2).

Now, this "hearing" of the gospel happened over days, weeks, months, even years. People were progressively exposed to the message as they chose to drop in on the church community and get more. Somewhere along the line, new spiritual birth would occur, but for some (just like today) they *could not point to a moment* when they were born anew. Instead, it was about a period of time in which they came to believe. Somewhere in that time frame, they were born of God's Spirit.

It's much like physical birth. I don't know about you, but I don't have any memories of being physically born. Still, I'm fairly certain it happened, as I've got a birth certificate to prove it! Likewise, I know loads of believers who have no recollection of a "salvation moment." They only know that they *began and then continued* to hear the message until, at some point, that spiritual birth took place.

Paul is saying it's important for the Colossians to *continue* hearing and believing. This is why the very next verse says, "This is the gospel that you heard and that has been proclaimed" (1:23). Just because something has been proclaimed and heard by people doesn't mean it has taken root in their lives yet! They need to *continue* to hear and believe in order to make sure they have grasped the gospel that saves.

This is the true meaning of the "continue" verses. They are certainly not designed to strike fear in a believer who has already been born of God's Spirit.

So, relax! We *cannot* lose our salvation.

Relax about Faith and Works!

"Yeah, but we've got to have a lot of works to be saved. James says that faith without works is dead" (see James 2:17). This sort of thinking can send some well-intentioned people into a tailspin of self-inspection: *Do I have enough works? Am I really saved?*

Let's face it. If these are the questions you're struggling with, then it's going to be pretty hard to relax with God.

The whole faith-works debate has been around a long time. Martin Luther even went so far as to say that the book of James shouldn't be in the Bible! The reason he had such a problem with it was that three times James says we are "justified by works." Let me repeat that in case you missed it—three times in chapter 2 James says we are "justified by works." Yes, verses 21, 24, and 25 all say "justified by

110

works" (NKJV). And there's really no getting around this reality, as the same Greek word, *dikaioō* ("justify"), is used in both James 2:24 ("justified by works") and in Romans 3:28 ("justified by faith").

James 2:24	"justified by works"
Romans 3:28	"justified by faith"

Now, this passage in James 2 *cannot* possibly be explained away as some sweet passage about a Christian lifestyle of works *after* salvation. No, justification before God is in focus, and the question being asked is, "Can that faith *save* him?" (v. 14 NASB). Clearly, the initial act of salvation itself is the topic.

To top it off, notice that verse 23 says, "Abraham believed God, and it was credited to him as righteousness." This verse helps us define "justified" in context. Justification here is when we believe and when righteousness is credited to us. This, of course, means *at salvation itself*. So James is clearly saying we're justified (made righteous) by "works"!

Works? Hang on. Don't tune me out yet. I'm a grace guy.

So what's going on here? I mean, are we justified (reckoned righteous before God) by works? Well, the answer to that question is, "Yes, but . . ." Yes, but we need to look to James 2 in order to see how James defines "works." So without further ado . . .

According to verse 21, what was Abraham justified by? Works. When? When he offered up Isaac. How many times did Abraham do this work? Once.

According to verse 25, what was Rahab justified by? Works. When? When she opened the door for the spies. How many times did Rahab do this work? Once.

So do you see it? In this case, "works" did not refer to a lifelong record of works that Abraham performed. It was not a series of works done over a lifetime as a result of his faith. No, it was *one* "work"—when he hoisted Isaac onto the altar. He believed God and then *responded*. In so doing, he was justified (i.e., righteousness was reckoned to him).

Similarly, this was not a lifelong record of works for Rahab either. It was not a series of works done over a lifetime as a result of her faith. No, it was *one* "work"—when she opened the door for the spies. She believed God and then *responded*. In so doing, she was justified (i.e., righteousness was reckoned to her).

With both Abraham and Rahab, their faith was "perfected" (v. 22 NASB) because it was accompanied by *response to God's message in the moment*. That's what "works" means here—response. So James is essentially saying that so-called faith in God's message without *response* to God's message is just dead faith. (Side note: Of course, good works are a natural, daily outflow of life in Christ, and many other passages speak of "works" in that way. My only point here is that we cannot impose that definition of "works" here in James 2, since daily works done over a lifetime do not justify and save us.)

If, when you heard the gospel, you responded by turning the doorknob and *opening* (like Rahab) the door of your heart and then *offering* (like Abraham) your life to be crucified with Christ, then you've already met the "works" requirement of James 2. You don't have to spend your life examining your works, tallying them up, and wondering if there's enough there to somehow prove your faith. No,

James never meant us to do any of that. The whole passage is simply about responding to the gospel message, which you've already done if you're in Christ. Now you can relax in the reality of your salvation, enjoying Jesus.

Final Thoughts

As we've seen, even the apostle James himself admits that "we all stumble in many ways" (3:2). So did James lose his salvation somewhere along the way because he didn't have enough works and stumbled too much? Of course not!

Everyone sins, a lot.

We all stumble in many ways. So how much is too much? When does God throw in the towel? The whole thing becomes silly as we remember that it's all about him, and it's *not* about us.

We need to keep in mind that "if we are faithless, he *remains faithful*, for he *cannot disown himself*" (2 Tim. 2:13) and that he says, "Never will I leave you; never will I forsake you" (Heb. 13:5) and "no one will snatch them out of my hand" (John 10:28). This truth begs us to *relax* with God.

And when it comes to that altogether different topic of *daily* good works, we can simply know that God has already prepared all of those for us anyway. We can wake up each day and walk right into them!

> *For we are His workmanship, created in Christ Jesus for good works, which God prepared beforehand so that we would walk in them. (Eph. 2:10 NASB)*

PART 3

RELAX IN THE
TRUTH
THAT SETS YOU
FREE

14

God Is Not Picking an Elite Few

"Heaven. Hell. Hell. Heaven. Hell." God goes down the city block selecting those who will believe in him? This idea has caused more controversy than nearly any other issue within Christianity. Throughout history, we've basically seen three main viewpoints on salvation: (1) God predestined you individually to believe and be saved; (2) you called upon the name of the Lord to be saved; or (3) they're both true, but you can't understand it until you get to heaven.

Some won't like how I opened this chapter—"Heaven. Hell. Hell. Heaven. Hell." They might say God doesn't pick anyone for hell. He only picks those headed to heaven. Still, this ends up looking like this: "Heaven." *Silence. Silence.* "Heaven." *Silence.* Note that the ones that God is silent about, by default, still go to . . . hell.

So is there *really* a big difference?

The predestination puzzle is admittedly a hard one to solve. We read a verse here. We read a verse there. And by the time we're done, we might end up convinced that God engages in individual preselection of those who will be saved.

Now, I believe God can do whatever he wants. After all, he is God, and we are not. I'm all for respecting the sovereignty of God. God calls the shots, period. I simply think we've missed the point of *what precisely God did choose* while exercising his authority.

Solving the predestination puzzle requires a bit of "working backward." A whole lot of unlearning needs to take place before we do any learning. What do I mean by that? The fact is that these days, so many of us have our Calvinist or Arminian glasses on that I'm not sure we can see very clearly.

The First Puzzle Pieces

When it comes to a passage like Romans 9—one of the landmark passages used to justify individual selection—we need to work backward, looking at Paul's conclusion first as a preview of coming attractions. So when Paul says, "What then shall we say?" (v. 30), you know it's time to perk up and pay attention. He is about to reveal the whole point of everything he's been saying. When Paul asks this, we should see it as a bright red indicator light flashing in our faces: "What then shall we say? *That the Gentiles*, who did not pursue righteousness, *have obtained it*, a righteousness that is *by faith*" (v. 30).

Bingo. That's it. That's the point. That Gentiles obtained righteousness by faith. That's precisely what Paul is defending in Romans 9—not the selection of you over your next-door neighbor. No, it's about God's sovereign selection of *Gentiles* to be included in the gospel.

So why is that such a big deal? Well, it's huge. "You mean to tell me that those dirty Gentiles (non-Jews), who could not care less about God, now get included in the gospel? Ridiculous!" Rewind two thousand years, and that was the typical Jewish reaction of the day.

See, many Jews felt that they "deserved" God. After all, worshiping Yahweh was in their lineage, their heritage, their history. But, c'mon, the Gentiles with their Vegas 2.0 lifestyle, their orgies, and their pagan temples and debauchery? There was no way that Yahweh should even give them a look. After all, when it came to the law, most Gentiles would be asking, "Moses who?"

They were so clueless.

So what if this whole predestination thing is really about God controversially preselecting those clueless Gentiles to receive the gospel too? Could it be that simple?

More Roman Pieces

An objection might be, "Yeah, but there's that part about God loving Jacob and hating Esau (Rom. 9:13). Then there's that part about Pharaoh being hardened (vv. 17–18), and then that other part about the potter having a right over the clay (v. 21). It seems like God is picking people, some for heaven and some for hell."

I hear what you're saying. But Paul is simply giving God's résumé as a person who does whatever he wants. In the

Old Testament, he said that the older (Esau) would serve the younger (Jacob). It could have been vice versa with the younger serving the older. But God called the shots. Now, Esau serving Jacob is not symbolic of Esau in hell and Jacob in heaven. It's not about heaven and hell. And it's not about lost versus saved. It's simply about God declaring who will serve whom. Again, it's about *God calling the shots*. That's the purpose of Paul citing the story.

"Yeah, but Romans talks about a hardening. Doesn't God harden people?" you might ask.

Jesus said, "I, when I am lifted up from the earth, will draw *all people* to myself" (John 12:32). So God is reaching out to *everyone*, and our role is to call upon the name of the Lord. It's a shame that God's own people historically (Israel) rejected him and that "Israel has experienced a hardening in part until the full number of the Gentiles has come in" (Rom. 11:25). But that was *Israel*. They experienced a *partial* hardening for a period of time. However, we shouldn't turn that into some doctrine about us going to heaven but the guy next door having no chance because God hardened him.

With the potter and clay analogy, the point is that *God can do whatever he wants*. After all, he's the potter! So he can use one piece of clay for honorable use and another piece for common use. He can make one thing for his trophy case and another for use at his kitchen table. He's the potter, and he calls the shots. So who are we to question him? Again, this is not about heaven and hell either. This is about the right of the potter to do whatever he wants, in general. Think about it. "For common use" (Rom. 9:21) would not be Paul's analogy for hell. No, "common use" refers to the status of one vessel compared with another vessel for honorable use. It's a reference to God doing whatever he wants *with the Gentiles*, despite the fact that Gentiles had a "dishonorable status" (common use) in Jewish society.

This is precisely why, in the midst of this discussion in Romans 9 about predestination and God's right to choose, we see Paul say, "not only from the Jews but also from the Gentiles" (v. 24). And then God says, "I will call them 'my people' who *are not my people*" (v. 25). Hello! This should be plain and obvious—predestination is that the Gentiles, who were not God's people, have now *also* been appointed to the gospel.

It's not complicated. It's not cruel. It's beautiful.

This was God's predestined choice that Paul was so adamantly defending. And it was directly related to Paul's apostleship to the Gentiles. This is why Paul goes on for chapters to thoroughly defend God's sovereign choice of the Gentile nations. After all, Paul was devoting his life to ministering to them. They'd better be included!

It was *never* about God handpicking individuals, some for heaven and others for hell. Under the new covenant, the breaking news was that even those dirty Romans, and even those dirty Ephesians, and today even those dirty Americans (hey, that's me!) are included in the gospel invitation.

The Ephesian Pieces

This is why when we flip over to Ephesians to study predestination, we find a peculiar use of *we/us* versus *you*.

Early in the letter, Paul is saying "we" were predestined, and then he goes on to say "you also" were included.

Who is the "we"? Jews.

Who is the "you also"? Gentiles.

See, it's a plural *you* (like a "y'all," as we say down South), and the point is that "we Jews" were always picked as God's chosen people. But now, under God's new way, "y'all Gentiles" are also included. Pull out a highlighter and work your way through the first two chapters of Ephesians, marking "we" and "you," and you'll discover the true meaning of predestination. Wait, let's make it even easier:

1:4	he chose *us* . . .
1:5	he predestined *us* . . .
1:12	*we*, who were *the first to put our hope in Christ*
1:13	and *you also* were included . . .
2:1	as for *you, you* were dead . . .
2:3	*all of us* also . . .
2:3	like the rest, *we* . . .
2:11	formerly *you who are Gentiles* by birth . . .
2:12–13	*you* were separate . . . far away . . .
2:14	[God] made *the two* groups one . . .
2:16	to reconcile *both* of them . . .
2:17a	peace to *you who were far away* . . .
2:17b	and peace to *those who were near* . . .
2:18	through him *we both* have access to the Father
2:19	*you* are no longer foreigners and strangers . . .
2:22	in him *you too* are being built together
3:1	for the sake of *you Gentiles*
3:6	*Gentiles* are heirs together with *Israel*

Key:
we/us = Jews
you (plural) = Gentiles
two/both = Jews and Gentiles together

Solving the Predestination Puzzle

Every time the word *you* shows up in the Bible, our temptation is to make it about us, individually. But here the word *you* is plural, and Paul means "y'all Gentiles." So what if predestination is not about you at the exclusion of your next-door neighbor? What if it's actually all about God's radical and controversial move to include the Gentiles in the gospel? I guess that'd mean that some of us have a whole lot of rethinking to do.

And while we're rethinking, consider this: Why isn't the doctrine of predestination taught in any comprehensive way in Hebrews, James, 1 Peter, 2 Peter, 1 John, 2 John, 3 John, or any epistle written to Jews?

Here's why: because the Jews *already* knew that Israel had been chosen. That was certainly not any new revelation for them! There was no need to teach Jews that they were picked. But it was the Gentiles who needed to know that they were now included! That's why we find predestination explicitly taught in both Ephesians and Romans—two letters to Gentiles. And that's why Paul is the only one to discuss it at length—because he was the apostle to the Gentiles.

Do you see why this is so important to straighten out? There's a flavor of the gospel out there that says God is going up and down the block shouting, "I'll take you and you and you, but to hell (literally) with the rest of you!" This sort of belief system inevitably leads some people to wonder, "Am I picked? I feel picked, but how can I know for sure?" This view of God makes it tough for many people to *relax* and enjoy God.

But here's a bit of truth to set you free: no matter whether you're a Jew or a Gentile, you were on God's mind as he made his new covenant moves on the cross and through the resurrection.

So relax—you're picked!

And *"everyone* who calls on the name of the Lord will be saved" (Rom. 10:13).

15

No One Can Obey
Those Teachings

If you're not careful, Jesus can really stress you out! Well, not Jesus himself. But what I call the "impossible teachings" of Jesus can certainly bring you to your knees in total exhaustion. I'm talking about when the Son of God starts telling his hearers to cut off their hands (Matt. 5:30), to pluck out their eyes (Matt. 5:29), to be perfect like God (Matt. 5:48), and to sell everything (Matt. 19:21). I'm talking about when he says that anger equals murder (Matt. 5:21–22) and looking with lust is the same as adultery (Matt. 5:27–28). Then to really heap it on, he says you'll be forgiven *if* you forgive others, but if you don't forgive other people, then you can forget it—you're toast (Matt. 6:14–15).

Ouch, that's going to leave a mark!

Yeah, Jesus can stress you out if you're not careful. Careful how? Well, you've got to be careful about the covenants. Otherwise, you will live in *covenantal confusion*.

Sure, a lot of people play around with the impossible teachings of Jesus. You know, they flirt with them. They don't cut off their hand or pluck out their eye or anything. Yet they walk around saying, "I'm a red-letter Christian." That means they supposedly live by *everything* that Jesus said to do in the four Gospels (his words are printed in red in some Bibles). But I've met some of these folks, and I can testify that not only are they not self-inflicted amputees, and not only are their eyes still firmly planted in their sockets, but they are not living perfectly like God (Matt. 5:48), and some of them are not very good at forgiving others in order to, in their minds, successfully secure their own forgiveness from God (Matt. 6:14–15).

As you journey through Matthew 5–6, you have to wonder: Cut off your hand? Pluck out your eye? Avoid anger? And no name-calling or else? With talk of animal sacrifices on altars and threats of hell for non-compliance along the way (Matt. 5:20, 22, 29, 30)? What's going on with these radical, impossible teachings of Jesus?

Covenantal Confusion

Jesus's impossible teachings in Matthew 5–6 are some of the harshest teachings one can find in any world religion. Why is that exactly? Does it mean that Christians should just try really, really hard to live out those teachings? Or is there something else going on here?

Fortunately, there's a simple answer. Jesus was born under the law and his audience was under the law too (Gal. 4:4–5). That's what Galatians 4 says, even though we might not hear that one in church very often. So Jesus wasn't preaching to a new covenant crowd when he said those harsh things. Instead, he was showing an old covenant crowd *why they desperately needed something different.*

The cross is the dividing line of human history. It's not baby Jesus lying in a manger in Bethlehem that changes everything. Hebrews says that *death*, not birth, brings a change of covenant (9:16–17). So for thirty-three years on planet Earth, Jesus was still living under the law with an audience that likewise was under the law. That's why you see him saying some pretty radical things that freaked people out, at least those who took him seriously. And yes, they were *supposed* to take him seriously!

So instead of explaining away Jesus's teachings by watering them down, I'm saying Jesus actually meant what he said. He presented an impossible standard (the spirit of the law) in order to absolutely bury people under hopelessness. That was the only way they'd see their need for a brand-new way of grace. Think about it: Unless you've faced the stringency of the law, why even entertain the idea that you need grace?

That's why Jesus looked on the rich man with such a deep love for him but then turned right around and told him to sell everything (Mark 10:21). Sell everything? Really? Is that the "plan of salvation" we promote today? Do we tell everybody to unload their stuff on Craigslist in order to reach heaven? Not at all! So why did Jesus tell a rich guy to hock his belongings? Why did Jesus pick the one thing the guy wouldn't do?

Jesus incited in him a sense of need, not hope.

That's what the law will do in all of us—point out where we fall short of the standard and show us why we need grace (Rom. 3:20). If the law hasn't done that to you yet, then maybe you haven't met the true spirit of the law!

Jesus can help you with that one—just start reading at Matthew 5:17, and let me know how it goes. Pay special attention to those parts about "the fire of hell" and being thrown into it (vv. 22, 29–30), because, contrary to popular opinion, Matthew 5:17–48 is not a sweet little passage about Christian growth!

The Great Divide

The new covenant (or *testament*—it's the same thing in Greek) doesn't really begin in Matthew 1. The Bible publishers dropped the ball when they put "The New Testament" in big block letters on that divider page right before Matthew 1 starts. Actually, the new covenant begins with Jesus's death, not his birth. Remember that a covenant doesn't start without blood (Heb. 9:18). That's why even the old covenant had to begin with Moses sprinkling animal blood all over the scroll and then, in graphic fashion, all over the people. Now, that's when you want to have a good umbrella handy!

So blood, not birth, starts a covenant. That's why we can say with confidence that the new covenant began at Calvary and not a day before. And that's why it makes all the sense in the world that *sometimes* (not all the time!) Jesus was trying to call people out concerning the true standard of the law. I guess some people thought they were doing just fine. Then Jesus opens his mouth to give his "killer sermon" in Matthew 5, and *boom*, reality hits.

They realize they stink at *real* righteousness.

Now, this doesn't mean that we take a Sharpie and start marking through a bunch of the Bible, saying, "I don't need to read that part." The whole Bible from Genesis to Revelation is the inspired Word of God. But it does mean that (1) we are *not under* the law and (2) we should therefore use discernment when Jesus refers to the law (Matt. 5:17, 21, 27) and then expounds upon its true and impossible standard of perfection.

That's all I'm saying.

And clearly this second point pertains to *only some*, not all, of Jesus's teachings. Before the cross, Jesus also prophesied about the new way to come and taught many, many things that are applicable to the church today—about the vine and the branches, the Holy Spirit, and the kingdom of God, to name a few among *many*!

Teach *Everything* Jesus Taught?

In Matthew 28:20, Jesus told his disciples to go out and teach *everything* that he told them to teach. So doesn't this mean that everything Jesus ever said is for us to try to obey today?

Well, when Jesus told the disciples to teach everything he had instructed them to teach, do you believe the disciples obeyed him? I do. And the epistles are the result of their obedience!

There's nothing missing in the epistles, yet where's the part about cutting off body parts, removing eyeballs, selling everything, anger equaling murder, and forgiving others first as the condition for being forgiven by God? These are entirely absent from the epistles. And in some cases we find teachings in the epistles that even directly oppose them! As we saw earlier, Ephesians 4:32 and Colossians 3:13 are great examples as they say we are to forgive others just as God *already* forgave us. So these two passages say the exact opposite of the forgive-to-be-forgiven teaching we find in Matthew 6:14–15!

No, the harsh law-based teachings of Jesus don't appear anywhere in the epistles, nor is there even anything remotely like them. So did James, Peter, John, and Paul drop the ball and forget to include those teachings? Maybe, just maybe, these impossible teachings about the true spirit of the law were *never what Jesus intended the disciples to teach* as doctrine to the New Testament church.

Now, that makes sense! That's why they are not carried over, after the cross. That's why they were not shared with the Galatians or the Ephesians or the Corinthians or any church for that matter. Those teachings are simply not part of the new covenant.

We don't amputate limbs. We don't strive to be perfect like God. We don't compare ourselves with the Pharisees and seek to exceed their righteousness. We don't live in fear of hell if we get angry with someone or call them a "fool" as Paul once did with "You foolish Galatians" (Gal.

3:1)! And we certainly don't try to forgive others in order to eventually earn forgiveness from God.

God's new covenant message of grace announces that we are forgiven not because we forgave others first, but because the blood of Jesus Christ was shed on our behalf. In him we have received total forgiveness as a gift from God. And it was our old self (not our hands or eyes) that was "cut off" (Col. 3:9) and then crucified with Christ (Rom. 6:6). The old self was then replaced as we were made new creations and filled and sealed with God's Spirit (Rom. 5:5; 2 Cor. 5:17; Eph. 4:30). Finally, we received perfection (righteousness) as a gift (Rom. 5:17), not through striving or comparing ourselves with religious leaders such as the Pharisees, but through "heart surgery" (Ezek. 36:26; Rom. 6:17). This is the new covenant in all of its glory, untainted by the law teachings with which Jesus intended to bury the Jews under condemnation.

In summary, Jesus never meant for the disciples to present those deadly "true spirit of the law" teachings to the New Testament church. After all, why would Jesus want to heap law on his own church that is now under grace? It would make no sense at all.

So when it comes to the impossible teachings of Jesus, you can just relax on *this* side of the cross with forgiveness and rightness with God being your free gift to enjoy!

16

It's Not about Water or Wine

Baptism. It's only a few seconds under the water, and yet a whole lifetime of debate can be stirred up by the topic!

Some say water baptism is essential to salvation. What? The guy who hears the gospel and believes it, but doesn't make it to the local swimming hole in time, he's out of luck?

The water worship has got to stop. There's nothing magical about H_2O that saves a guy. Sure, it's a wonderful picture of being immersed in and saturated with new life in Jesus Christ. Baptism represents that to a crowd as they watch you act out your own spiritual death by going down into the water and then portray your own spiritual resurrection as you rise up out of the water.

But let's leave it at that.

This business about *needing* to be baptized in order to be saved is crazy talk. The thief on the cross would certainly agree with me (Luke 23:39–43)! And don't forget about those guys who received the Holy Spirit in Acts 10:47 and then *later* were water baptized. Peter says this about them: "Surely no one can stand in the way of their being baptized with water. They have received the Holy Spirit just as we have" (Acts 10:47). That certainly shows us something! Water baptism doesn't save. Water baptism doesn't give us the Spirit. Water baptism is simply a way to commemorate what already happened. It's another instance of "do this in remembrance of me" (Luke 22:19).

A birthday party doesn't mean you're being born. An anniversary doesn't mean you're getting married. And baptism doesn't mean you're getting saved. They're all merely celebrations of what *already* took place. That is why Paul puts it so plainly to the Corinthians: *"For Christ did not send me to baptize*, but to preach the gospel—not with wisdom and eloquence, lest the cross of Christ be emptied of its power" (1 Cor. 1:17). Look, if baptism were a requirement for salvation, then wouldn't Paul have been sent to baptize too? But obviously it's the "preach the gospel" part that saves, not baptism in water.

It's pretty clear that water baptism is not something we must do in order to receive the Spirit. Galatians 3 says we receive the Spirit by believing what we hear (the gospel; Rom. 10:17), not by any ceremony performed. On top of that, 1 Peter 3:21 says that water baptism does not save us, but instead it's all about being baptized spiritually into Christ's resurrection!

The simple fact is that there's nothing on Earth that can save us. No earthly act can bring us the Spirit. He does not indwell us by water or by any other liquid, for that matter. No, the only thing that really "works" is being baptized *into Christ himself* when we believe the gospel (Rom. 6:3–4). This is precisely why Jesus said that John baptized with water but that the new way would be baptism with the Holy Spirit (Acts 1:5).

So by all means, relax and enjoy the birthday party, but let's not act like we're just being born!

The Lord's Supper

Speaking of rituals, what's up with the way we're celebrating the Lord's Supper?

Have you noticed that, at least in some places, they're dimming the lights and things get kind of somber? Sometimes, there's crying and even some wailing. I realize that people can get sad over their many sins, their regrets, and the ways they've failed. But it seems like we're into celebrating our guilt more than celebrating our God! After all, didn't he say to do the whole thing "in remembrance of" him (1 Cor. 11:25)? It seems like we can get so infatuated with our sins that sometimes we lose sight of our Savior!

I've tried to track down exactly what's happening in some of these churches—why we're sometimes invited to an orgy of self-examination rather than a celebration of Jesus. I think it may come down to a misunderstanding of one verse in 1 Corinthians 11 where Paul says to a specific group of Corinthian believers, "Everyone ought to examine themselves" (v. 28). And with those five words, Christians today bolt into self-evaluation mode the moment they see the bread and wine coming down the aisle.

Here's the thing about that verse, though. We were never supposed to turn it into some examination ritual before celebrating in remembrance of Jesus. No, it was meant to treat a *specific problem in one church* in Corinth two thousand years ago. There were divisions and a lot of bitterness going on in that church (v. 18).

Back then, the Lord's Supper was celebrated with a complete meal, and some were showing up early and eating up all the food. And don't think for a minute that the wine wasn't disappearing early too! Yeah, it was gluttony and drunkenness that was the problem (vv. 20–22). In fact, the issue was so pervasive that, from these drinking binges, people were getting sick, and passing out, and maybe some were even dying of alcoholism (v. 30). I'm not sure any of this can happen today since most of us celebrate the Lord's Supper by ingesting just enough Welch's grape juice to fill a thimble, along with a crouton-sized morsel of bread!

Now, remember, it's Corinth. Picture Vegas plus spring break plus Mardi Gras on steroids. To top it off, poor people were showing up, and there was nothing left for them to eat at the church potluck. This is why Paul's whole solution to the matter was for them to *wait for one another* and then *eat together*. If anyone was super hungry, they were supposed to eat at home before showing up (vv. 33–34). That way, people wouldn't end up arguing over cupcakes and casting judgment on each other at what was supposed to be a celebration of the body and blood of Jesus!

So what did Paul want them to "examine" (v. 28)? Well, it's pretty obvious in light of all that was happening! He was saying, "Stop and consider what you're doing. If you're showing up early, eating up all the food, getting drunk and passing out, and leaving nothing for the poor, then take time to examine your actions. Reevaluate whether you're honoring Jesus with the way you're handling this. And by all means, wait for your brothers and sisters in Christ, so that they can enjoy the meal along with you. It's about community and unity!"

That was the examination needed, not some sort of dim-the-lights, morbid introspection of all the sins they'd recently committed. It was never meant to elicit an obsession with confession. And it never had anything to do with trying to "qualify" for the Lord's Supper. Remember that we are *already* qualified because of the blood of Jesus and nothing else.

So when you celebrate, are you thinking about your sins or your Savior? Are you consumed with a greatness of guilt or the greatness of God? Have you thought about what you're fixated on during the Lord's Supper?

Let us fix our eyes on Jesus, the author and perfecter of our faith, who for the joy set before him endured the cross, scorning its shame, and sat down at the right hand of the throne of God. (Heb. 12:2 NIV 1984)

What about Matthew 5?

Some people have used Matthew 5 to perpetuate the whole confess-to-qualify thing right before the Lord's Supper. It's the chapter where Jesus is talking about getting right with someone. Jesus says, "Therefore, if you are offering your gift *at the altar* and there remember that your brother or sister has something against you, leave your gift there in front of *the altar*. First go and be reconciled to them; then come and offer your gift" (vv. 23–24).

First, none of the apostles ever say anything remotely like this in the context of the Lord's Supper. And why would they? I mean, can you imagine us getting up and walking out of the church service, going to find somebody we've offended, and then coming back later to celebrate the Lord's Supper after we "got right" with someone?

(Side note: Don't forget that this verse in Matthew 5 is only a few verses away from the "cut off your hand" and "pluck out your eye" verses. That's something to consider, as we can't exactly go multiple choice on which verses we want to apply from this passage!)

On top of that, it's pretty clear what Jesus's real meaning was—he was talking to Jewish people about their offerings on *altars*. Today, there are no altars. *The cross replaced all the Old Testament altars.* (No, that table at the front of the church is not an altar!) Not to mention, we aren't making any offerings to God at the Lord's Supper. It's actually vice versa, as we are celebrating Jesus's offering for us! So it's simply an unsound practice to reach back to Matthew 5 and start teaching Christians that we need to "get right" with others before we celebrate with the bread and the wine.

Now, I am all for living "at peace with everyone" (Rom. 12:18). But when it comes to the moment of celebrating the Lord's Supper, we should realize that we are *already* at peace with God because of Jesus.

We really can sit back, *relax*, and enjoy!

17

You Don't Owe God Money

Money.

Money breaks up marriages. Money turns people off to church. Money is one of the most controversial subjects on the planet, right up there with religion and politics.

Tithing only makes it all the more controversial. Of course, tithing is the idea that God wants 10 percent of your income. (Now, the true percentage in the Old Testament, when you add it all up, is a bit over 20 percent, and whether that is gross or net remains unclear!)

So, are you robbing God?

We've all heard that one. And nothing turns my stomach more. I mean, let me get this straight—we're supposed to picture God up in heaven desperately craving our money, and when we don't fork over at least 10 percent of it, he gets mad? Some say he withholds blessings like a slot machine that withholds your winnings if you don't keep pumping

enough quarters in. Others say he not only withholds blessings but curses you too!

Pressure. Manipulation. The sly tactics never cease. I
know of one church that has you come down to the front
during the service to give your tithe. The only catch (in addition to everyone watching you) is that you're supposed
to label your gift with a colored envelope. You know, black
for a standard gift, silver for a big gift, and gold for a huge
gift. You come marching down the aisle with envelope in
hand, while the crowd cheers you on. And everybody knows
exactly what size gift you're giving (or you simply learn to
lie). Sure, you can stay in your seat and give nothing, but you
start getting that uneasy, guilty feeling . . . right on schedule.

Is this the sort of thing that God wants for us? When the
apostle Paul heard that one church was going to give him
a monetary gift, you know what he did? He sent someone
else on ahead of him, someone less intimidating, to receive
the gift (2 Cor. 9:5). Why did he do that? So that the church
wouldn't feel pressure to give beyond their means and then
give grudgingly. Now, that's a gentleman. That's a heart
of sensitivity. And it seems to be the polar opposite of the
pressure tactics we see in some of today's churches.

Buying Blessings?

Don't get me wrong. I'm all for giving freely and generously
so that the gospel message gets out there and people grow
in Christ. I'm sold out to it! But when pastors start pulling
verses from Malachi about storehouses and grain offerings and blessings and curses (Mal. 3:8–10), that's where

I jump ship. Then some throw in the part about how God is going to pay back tithers threefold (or fivefold if you go to the church down the street!). That's when I start asking if their ministry will write a check to my ministry so they can receive the fivefold back from God themselves! Is that too much to ask?

The latest thing these days seems to be a "money-back guarantee" on your tithe. A quick internet search reveals that loads of churches are going that direction. Here's how it works: If you're not satisfied with the amount of blessings or payback you receive within the three months that follow your tithes, then no worries—you can approach the church leadership and get your money back. The only catch is that you've got to be the one to say, "Um, yeah, it didn't work for me, so I was wondering if I could get the money back now."

Awkward! And that's the whole point, I think. Who is going to actually try to claim their refund? Only the few, the bold, and the desperate. So the numbers likely work out well for any church pushing the money-back guarantee.

I don't know. Should we really be telling God, "Hey, I'm going to drop this money in the offering plate, and if you don't bless me back within the time limit that Pastor Rick set, then I'm going to be asking for it back, as per our agreement"?

It just seems off. I mean, there's no back-out plan for giving a conditional gift to God that I see in Scripture, and I certainly don't see where God honors these sorts of "deals" we supposedly make with him.

You'll also often hear that we need to give "until it hurts," whatever that means. Some will try to tell you that unless it's a painful sacrifice, you're not giving what you should. Huh? Really? But 2 Corinthians 8:12–14 talks about giving *cheerfully* because we see people in need and because we've got an abundance of money *to spare* and we want to further the gospel. Apparently, giving is supposed to feel good, not hurt!

The Root of Tithing

This whole 10 percent required tithe comes straight out of the Jewish law. Jesus himself affirms this as he chastises the Pharisees, saying: "Woe to you, *teachers of the law* and Pharisees, you hypocrites! You give a tenth of your spices—mint, dill and cumin. But you have neglected *the more important matters of the law*—justice, mercy and faithfulness. You should have practiced the latter, without neglecting the former" (Matt. 23:23). Notice that here Jesus refers to tithing as a matter of the law that is compared with other "more important matters of the law."

Yes, according to the law, Israel was required to support their priests with 10 percent (and then some!) of their income in addition to giving various other tithes. But those priests weren't allowed to own property or have any belongings of their own, and they weren't allowed to work outside of their priestly duties. Yet today we find pastors and church leaders who are demanding that same 10 percent from churchgoers, and meanwhile they own homes and cars and even hold down second and third jobs as seminary professors, authors, Bible dieticians, prayer rug vendors, and so on.

It just doesn't add up.

Don't forget that we Gentiles were never even given the Jewish law to start with (Rom. 2:14)! Ephesians tells us that we Gentiles had no covenant and no hope at all until God's new way came on the scene (2:12). So what in the world are we doing over here on the west side of the Atlantic, thousands of miles from Israel, as Gentiles, pushing a 10 percent tithe and quoting from Malachi 3 about curses and blessings?

Note that some do skip over the curse part altogether, because it's likely too "ecclesiastically incorrect" these days to tell people in church that they're cursed. So these teachers focus exclusively on the promise of blessing if you bring the whole tithe "into the storehouse" (Mal. 3:10). (I've often imagined pulling up to one of these churches with a dump truck full of grain and dumping it on their lawn. Too much?)

Does it even strike us as odd that *not one single New Testament epistle contains any single verse of instruction for us to tithe 10 percent*? Did the apostles somehow overlook such an important teaching?

Let's get with the program—it's about *freedom* in our giving.

The Truth about Mel

Now, often when looking through the New Testament epistles, somebody will bring up that one Old Testament story recounted in Hebrews 7 about Abraham giving a tenth to Melchizedek. So let's keep in mind a few things:

1. It's an Old Testament story recounted for a specific reason.

2. There are no "application" verses in the passage telling us to tithe 10 percent.
3. It was spoils of war that Abraham gave to Melchizedek.

That's right. Abraham went to battle, slaughtered people, took their belongings, and then offered a tenth of his *spoils of war* to Mel (vv. 1–2). Are we actually supposed to imitate that one? Can you imagine us warring against other religious groups and then hauling our plunder over to the local church? Do I even have to go there?

Giving 10 percent of your spoils of war was a common practice after battle in the Middle East. It was a sign of respect for authority. This Old Testament story was retold in Hebrews for a specific reason. Here's the logic of Hebrews 7:

1. Abe represents Levi. Mel represents Christ.
2. Abe is lesser than Mel. Levi is lesser than Christ.
3. The priest of the old covenant is lesser than the priest of the new covenant.
4. The old covenant is lesser than the new covenant.
5. Therefore, the new covenant is superior.

That is the point. That's the whole reason the story is retold. It's about two priests being compared and two covenants being compared. No other point is being made in the passage.

What about the Four Gospels?

But what about in the four Gospels? Doesn't Jesus tell us to tithe?

Well, not really, unless you're a Pharisee. There are only three passages in the Gospels that even mention the tithe.

Again, Matthew 23:23 and Luke 11:42 show Jesus chastising the Pharisees for tithing their spices but neglecting weightier matters of the law like justice and mercy. And in the third passage, Luke 18:11–14, Jesus addresses an egotistical Pharisee who is bragging about how he is not like evildoers and faithfully pays his tithes.

That's it for mentions of tithing in the Gospels. So unless you're a Pharisee under the Jewish law, you won't find any instruction from Jesus to tithe. In the four Gospels, there are no mandates for the New Testament church to tithe, at all.

Freedom. That's the takeaway here.

Freedom means we live from our hearts when it comes to loving people and when it comes to giving money. Freedom should define every aspect of our lives! Second Corinthians says that wherever the Spirit of God is, he marks his territory by fostering an environment of liberty (3:17). This doesn't mean that we sit on our wallets and yell "freedom" all the time. It simply means we get to be motivated by God's Spirit to give what he lays on our hearts, freely and without pressure, but also generously as he inspires us (2 Cor. 9:7). This might be 3 percent or 10 percent or 18 percent, and sometimes it might mean we give nothing at all, if there is good reason.

God doesn't need our money. Acts says that he doesn't need anything at all from us (17:25). Remember, he is God and he *already* owns everything! So let's ditch the idea that we owe God and that we are robbing him when we don't pay "enough" at church. That's just guilt theology in action. Instead, as we work our way through 2 Corinthians 8 and 9, we discover that we can give *cheerfully* when we see a *need*, when we are *excited* about the ministry, and when we have *extra* to give (8:12–14; 9:7).

This is very different from telling the single mother of five who is barely squeaking by on $15,000 a year that she needs to shell out at least $1,500 to her local church or she is robbing God. It's also very different from telling her the lie that if she does give her $1,500 this year, she'll get it back (with heavenly interest) within a time limit of three months! Paul describes people who push such ludicrous ideas as "people of corrupt mind, who have been robbed of the truth and who think that godliness is a means to financial gain" (1 Tim. 6:5). Enough said.

So relax and enjoy giving from your heart, all the while remembering that *you don't owe God*. God himself has announced that through the cross he canceled all law-based indebtedness to him and thereby disarmed anyone who might accuse us:

> Having canceled the charge of our legal indebtedness, which stood against us and condemned us; he has taken it away, nailing it to the cross. And having disarmed the powers and authorities, he made a public spectacle of them, triumphing over them by the cross. (Col. 2:14–15)

Epilogue

Relaxing with God

Wow! We've celebrated so many amazing truths within the new covenant. How radical they are! And how life-changing they can be for anyone who chooses to *relax* in them. My hope is that you'll rejoice together with me in how brilliant our God is in designing such a glorious covenant. And my prayer is that you have now seen the wide-open doorway to fully relaxing with God. But just in case, let's revisit some of the main attractions from our journey together!

Relax: You're Free!

New Testament believers shouldn't have any spiritual relationship with the law. The law serves only one purpose today: it shows the unbeliever their need for Christ. Once in Christ, we're no longer under the supervision of the law.

The law is a ministry of condemnation that brings death. The law was introduced so that sins would increase before our very eyes, not decrease. If anyone is under the law (while lost or saved), it will arouse sinful passions. The power of sin is experienced in law-based living (1 Cor. 15:56). But apart from the law, sin loses its grip on us (Rom. 7:8).

Those led by the Spirit have no business being under the law. It's ludicrous to even suggest such a thing! It would mean that Christians should refrain from eating shellfish and pork sandwiches. Christian women would need to remain "in the tent" during that time of the month. And clothing spun from more than one linen would need to be thrown out. We don't fully realize what we're saying when we sign up for obedience to the law.

Some say we're free from the Levitical regulations and the sacrificial system, but we're still under the Ten Commandments. If this were true, we'd need to abide by the Sabbath, abstaining from those Friday night emails and that Saturday yard work. But being under the Ten alone isn't really an option anyway. We're not given the right to dice up God's law (613 regulations!) into segments in order to adopt some but not all of it.

The law is an all or nothing proposition. James reminds us that whoever keeps the whole law and only stumbles in one point is guilty of all of it. Galatians reminds us that those under the law are under a curse, because you're cursed if you don't do *everything* written in the law. This is precisely why God freed us from *all* requirements of the law, not just some of them.

As unbelievers, we were "married" to the requirements of the law. But as Christians, we died to the law, so that we might be remarried to the risen Christ. For us a return to the law as a means of salvation *or as a guide for daily living* is spiritual adultery. We're cheating on Jesus, who is all we need for life and godliness. The fruit of his Spirit expressed through us is sufficient for every good work. So to rely on commandments engraved on stone reveals that our confidence in the indwelling Christ is nonexistent or pitiful at best. *We're saying we'll take Jesus for his blood but not for his resurrection life in us.*

In highlighting the power of God's grace, we don't devalue the law. Instead, we place the law on a pedestal and honor it as being perfect in every way. We admit that it's so perfect and so demanding that we can't possibly meet its sterling standard. For that very reason, God freed us from the law and offered us a totally different system for relating to him. Thank God that we're liberated from a system that only promotes failure.

Thank God for the beauty of his new covenant way!

Relax: You're Forgiven!

Christians aren't being forgiven progressively. We're forgiven people! Our forgiveness isn't dependent upon our ability to remember every single sin and confess it or ask for forgiveness. No, our cleansing came through the blood of Christ alone. It's based on his finished work, not on our keeping short accounts with God. "Once for all" forgiveness, as Hebrews 10:10 puts it, is the incredible benefit we enjoy on this side of the cross.

So forgiveness isn't something that we continually ask for, plead for, beg for, or wait for. The phrases "ask forgiveness" and "ask for forgiveness" are entirely absent from the epistles. Why? Because asking for forgiveness certainly doesn't take into account the *finished* work of Christ. We don't ask, over and over, for what we already have!

Christ Jesus will never die again. His blood will never be shed for our sins again. Since his blood was the catalyst that brought us total forgiveness for all our sins, we're urged to bank on the idea that no repeat is needed. There's no other sacrifice for sins, since his one and only perfect sacrifice was enough. When we add any condition to our forgiveness, we spit on the Son of God.

Think about it. If there were a daily system for getting more forgiveness and cleansing, then the Galatians, Ephesians, Philippians, Colossians, Corinthians, and Thessalonians apparently never heard about it! Why didn't they? Because a cleansing ritual makes no sense in light of the sufficiency of Christ's blood to remove all of our sins, once and forever.

Imagine the potential impact on the guilt-ridden if the church today were to drop their inconsistent and unbiblical belief systems about forgiveness. What if we were to simply agree with the God of the universe that "it is finished" (John 19:30)?

Relax: You're New!

Salvation is way more than getting a bit of "whipped cream" of the Holy Spirit on top of our old self. When we place our faith in Christ, a surgery takes place at the very center of our being. In Christ, we receive a new human spirit and God's Spirit within us.

We participate in Christ's death, burial, and resurrection. We die and start all over with a new spiritual lineage. We're different at the core. It's not merely that our value system changes, nor that God's Spirit comes to live within us. It's more. Our own human spirit (which was dead to God) is exchanged for a new human spirit. This is the most impacting change that can occur in anyone. It's literally becoming someone else spiritually.

But if our old self is dead, then why do we still get those nagging thoughts swirling through our mind? Shouldn't we be sin-free if we're so new? Although the old self has been killed off, the flesh is still present and active. The flesh is a network of worldly strategies for living that we employ to get our needs met. But the flesh is not our spiritual nature. The flesh is not who we are. Remember that it's like out-of-date software that's still running on our new spiritual hardware. Although we are sometimes tempted to resort to a fleshly means of getting by, we aren't designed to walk that way. It will never fulfill. In fact, walking after the flesh goes against our new nature and is incompatible with our spiritual design.

But the flesh doesn't work alone. It's in cahoots (that's Southern talk) with a power called *sin* that accesses our minds through the physical brain. This secret agent, sin, is cold and calculating in its attempt to sway us toward dependency on the flesh. It's crafty in that it serves us tailor-made temptation to appeal directly to the flavors of flesh we struggle with. Paul even went so far as to say that when this sin parasite was engaged, Paul was no longer in control of his actions. He was feeling like a slave to *something else* (Rom. 7:17, 20)!

Recognizing these sources of temptation (the flesh and the power of sin) is essential to a proper understanding of our spiritual identity—who we really are! Otherwise, the waters get murky. *Am I righteous or sinful? Am I a saint or a sinner? What does my heart truly desire? And why am I getting these thoughts all the time?*

Questions like these can't accurately be answered unless we can biblically account for our everyday thought lives in a clear way. Once the real nature of the battle is exposed, we can more easily grasp the life-changing truth that we're aliens in this world, literally born of the Spirit, and redesigned from the ground up for good works. We can stop living under the delusion that we are a "household divided against itself" (Matt. 12:25)!

Here's the bottom line: now that you're in Christ, there's nothing wrong with you! You're accepted, because God fashioned you into someone acceptable to him. You're called righteous, because you've literally and actually been re-created as a holy, righteous saint at your core. In your spirit, you're 100 percent new because of what he did *for* you and *to* you.

Your attitudes and actions are impacted not through fleshly effort, but through remembering the "heart surgery" and banking on it as reality in the moment. So how is the Christian life lived?

Step 1: Learn who you are in Jesus Christ.

Step 2: Wake up and be yourself.

Step 3: Repeat.

Now, how's that for a three-step program?

Relax: You've Got Resurrection Life!

Christianity isn't merely a free trip to heaven; nor does it primarily concern studying a religious book; nor is it centrally about reforming one's attitudes and actions. Although heaven, Bible study, and behavior are aspects of the Christian life that play an important role, they're not the main reason that Christ came. In his own words, Jesus said plainly, "I have come that they may have life" (John 10:10).

Salvation is nothing short of possessing Christ's life within our physical shell. Yes, just beneath your flesh and bones and all of what you've called "you"—that is where Jesus literally and actually lives!

And the new spiritual life we possess through Christ grants us long-term security. We'll be saved as long as Christ's own life endures. It's by God's initiative that we're in Christ Jesus. Therefore, it's up to him to keep us in Christ. God promised that the same Person who began this good work in us will carry us on to completion. He'll never leave us nor forsake us, and no one can snatch us out of his hand. These promises allow us to walk through life with confidence. We're united with Christ, and nothing can separate us from his love.

Carrying the Spirit of Christ within us is not a new concept. It's simply the restoration of life that Adam and Eve lost in the Garden. So Christianity is not a behavior improvement program nor even a religion in the strictest sense. It's more fundamentally natural than that. Christianity is a human's nature being returned to its innocent (righteous) state and the Spirit of God being restored to his rightful place within us.

This is the real thing in all of its potency. This is the message that the early church was willing to be persecuted and killed for. Jesus Christ literally and actually living within you, no matter what. Jesus Christ turning the mundane into miracle, each and every day. Jesus Christ not rearranging your circumstances but being new life to you, even in the midst of old circumstances.

Now, *that* is powerful.

Relax: It's the Way to Truly Live!

The freedom, forgiveness, identity, and new life that we possess through the new covenant are not affected in any way by our daily performance. These treasures are ours to keep.

In short, grace is grace, no matter what.

But in the Scriptures, there seem to be two reoccurring reasons for choosing upright behavior: (1) good works fit with who we are by nature now as saints; and (2) good works are the most sensible choice, since sinning is never profitable anyway. The new covenant that saved us, secured us, and gave us a future is the same covenant that teaches us to say no to sin. But even when we manage to say no to sin, we still need the means to say yes to good works.

That too happens through resting in the truths of new covenant grace.

From spiritual birth to spiritual growth, it's all about fixing your eyes on the finished work of Jesus Christ. In so doing, Jesus promises "rest for your souls" (Matt. 11:29).

Isn't it time you started relaxing with God?

Relaxing with God

A Seven-Part Study Experience

Part 1—Relax: There's a New Way

1. Read Hebrews 9:16–17. The words *covenant, will,* and *testament* were used interchangeably in the original language. When did the new covenant actually begin? Why do you think this might be important to consider as we study the Bible?

2. Read Hebrews 8:8–12. How does God describe the new covenant? What are the characteristics of it? How does each aspect of the covenant fit together to make a comprehensive whole that is not "cheap grace" or "dangerous," as some might think?

3. Read Hebrews 10:8–10. What did God do with the first covenant? What does this new "will" (covenant) do for us? Is it expressed in present, past, or future tense? Will it ever need to be amended or repeated?

4. Read Hebrews 7:18–19. Why was the former regulation set aside? What makes the new covenant any different?

5. Read Hebrews 8:13. How is the old covenant described? Why is it seen in this light now?

6. Read Hebrews 8:7–8. The law is holy and perfect, so what was the *real* problem with the old covenant?

7. Read Hebrews 7:11–12. God could have had Jesus be born into the lineage of Levi and Aaron. What point was God making by having Jesus born outside that Old Testament priestly line?

8. Read Hebrews 8:6. How are the old and new covenants compared? Why are they so different?

9. Read Hebrews 9:15. How is Christ's priesthood described? How is our inheritance described? What about believers who were under the old covenant?

Part 2—Relax: There's a New Priest in Town

1. Read Hebrews 7:20–22. What oath was involved in the new covenant? Who promised whom? What does this mean for us?

2. Read Hebrews 7:23–25. How is Jesus's priesthood different from the old covenant priests'? How is our salvation described here? What does this passage say is the reason that we are saved forever?

3. Read Hebrews 10:1–3. How often were old covenant sacrifices made? How effective were they? If Old Testament people had what we enjoy today, what would have been the two results?

4. Read Hebrews 10:3–5. What role did Old Testament sacrifices actually play in the conscience? Did they *take away* sins or simply cover (and atone) for them?

5. Read Hebrews 9:26–28. Why do you think the number of times Christ died is emphasized here? What does this mean for your forgiveness? What does it say about the return of Christ?

6. Read John 1:29; 1 John 2:1–2; and 1 John 3:5. What did Jesus accomplish that old covenant sacrifices did not?

7. Read Hebrews 1:3 and 10:11–14. What do standing and sitting represent in these passages? Which "position" are you in concerning your sins? What did Jesus's one sacrifice accomplish? For how long?

8. Read Hebrews 10:17–18. What is God's attitude now toward our sins? What tense is our forgiveness expressed in—past, present, or future? What does it mean to you that Jesus will never make another sacrifice for your sins ever again?

9. Read Hebrews 4:1, 9–11. What is the promise that still stands? How do you think we can "make every effort" to rest? What brings us this spiritual rest?

10. Read Hebrews 4:16 and 10:19–23. How should we feel in God's presence? What is the reason we can feel this way? Finally, why can we have such an incredible hope?

Part 3—Relax: You're Not Under Law

1. Read 1 Timothy 1:5–10. What problem does Paul inform the young pastor Timothy about? Who is the law actually made for?

2. Read Romans 3:19–20. Who is the law speaking to? What is it saying? What is the result in the conscience?

3. Read Galatians 3:19–24. What does the law tell the world? When were we prisoners of the law? What purpose did the law serve at that time? How?

4. Read Galatians 2:16. What does Paul say that he and his fellow apostles know? What was their decision as a result?

5. Read Galatians 3:21. Do the law and the promises of God conflict? Why or why not? What comes by the promise that the law can never achieve?

6. Read Matthew 5:21–22, 27–29. In what ways is Jesus raising the bar and exposing the true spirit of the law? What do you think was the reaction among his hearers in that day? Do you think we are any more capable of keeping that standard today?

7. Read Galatians 3:10 and James 2:10. Is God grading our best efforts on a curve under the law? How is being under the law described? How does this sound to you?

8. Read Romans 6:14 and 7:5, 8. What two things happen to sin under a law system? How is freedom from sin enjoyed?

9. Read Colossians 2:20–23. Who is Paul speaking to— believers or unbelievers? What does Paul say about a rules-based system? Why do you think that we can afford to live in this liberating way?

10. Read 2 Corinthians 3:7–9. Some people think that the Ten Commandments are still the "source" or the "goal" in focus for Christians today. How does this

verse describe the Ten Commandments? What evidence is there that the Ten Commandments are specifically being described here? How is God's alternative for us described?

11. Read Galatians 4:4–5. Was Jesus born into a time of law or a time of grace? What about his audience? What might this mean for the way in which we look at some of Jesus's harshest teachings about amputating body parts and trying to be perfect? What do you think Jesus's motive was in teaching such things to that audience?

Part 4—Relax: You're Under Grace

1. Read Matthew 5:17–18. Have heaven and earth disappeared yet? Therefore, has the law been abolished? Has the law been fulfilled? If the law has been fulfilled, are we supposed to "help God" fulfill it today? If that's not the goal, what do you think is the goal of the Christian life?

2. Read Romans 8:3–4. When did God fulfill the law? How did God fulfill the law? To what extent did he fulfill the law? What does this mean for the idea of us trying to fulfill the law today?

3. Read Romans 10:4. What does it say about the law? What does it say about righteousness?

4. Read Galatians 3:24–25. What purpose did the law serve? Now that we are believers, what role should the law have in our lives?

5. Read Galatians 5:18. How is our relationship to the law described? What is God's alternative for us?

6. Read Romans 7:4–6. What happened to our connection to law-based living? To whom do we belong? What had to take place for us to truly bear fruit? How do we serve now?

7. Read Galatians 2:19. What was the experience Paul had to go through in order to truly live for God?

8. Read Galatians 3:1–3. Here Paul gives the Galatians a multiple-choice test of sorts. What two things does he ask them? How do these two questions relate to each other? Should we have different answers to each?

9. Read Galatians 5:2–4. What happens to a person who opts for law-based living? What is the true standard for them? Does anyone achieve that standard? What phrases are used to describe those who try to "get right with God" by law?

10. Read Titus 2:11–14. According to this passage, what two things does the grace of God do? Does it sound to you like God thinks that a life under grace is "risky" when it comes to behavior?

11. Read 2 Corinthians 12:9. Does living under grace leave you powerless? What is our attitude and God's response that enables life under grace to really "work"?

12. Read Galatians 5:1. What did Christ do for us? How important is it to preserve the purity of the message?

Part 5—Relax: You're Forgiven

1. Read Colossians 2:13–14. What three things did God do for us in the new covenant?

2. Read Ephesians 4:32 and 1 John 2:12. What tense is our forgiveness expressed in—past, present, or future? What does this mean for you personally?

3. Read John 3:17–18 and Romans 8:1–2. What are we told about being judged or condemned? What is the cause for our freedom from judgment?

4. Read Ephesians 1:7 and Colossians 1:13–14. What two things are given to us in Christ? Why is it so important to see that we can't have one without having the other?

5. Read Romans 5:11 and Colossians 1:21–22. What does it mean to you to be fully reconciled to God? In the Colossians passage, what three phrases are used to describe you?

6. Read 2 Corinthians 5:18–19. Now that we've been reconciled, what ministry have we been given? What is the message we can share?

7. Read John 19:30. What do Jesus's final words on the cross mean to you personally?

8. Read 1 John 1:8–10. This passage has popularly been seen as a "bar of soap" for Christians to achieve daily cleansing. But in verse 8, what was the claim people were making in that day? And in verse 10, how is this claim expressed another way? Can we be true believers in Christ yet claim sinless perfection in our performance? So how is verse 9 the life-changing solution for unbelievers making such a ridiculous claim?

9. Read Matthew 6:14–15. This is the conclusion to what is commonly called "the Lord's Prayer." What is the condition for God forgiving us? Compare this with

Ephesians 4:32 and Colossians 3:13. Think in terms of the "cart" (us forgiving others) and the "horse" (God forgiving us). Which comes first in each passage? Why is there a difference in what the passages are saying?

Part 6—Relax: You're New on the Inside

1. Read Romans 5:12, 15 and 1 Corinthians 15:22. How did sin enter into the world? What "location" is the cause of our spiritual death?

2. Read 1 Corinthians 1:30 and Colossians 1:13. What is our new spiritual "location"? What benefits do we gain there?

3. Read Romans 6:3–6. List at least five different results of being spiritually placed *into* Christ. What do these mean to you in terms of how you view yourself, temptation, and your closeness with God?

4. Read Ephesians 2:5–6. List at least three different benefits of being *in* Christ. Is heaven *only* a future destination for you? How might this passage affect your answer?

5. Read Colossians 3:3–4. What exactly happened to you spiritually at salvation? Where is your life now? Who is your life now? What does your new spiritual location mean to you in terms of your security?

6. Read 1 Corinthians 1:26. What three different words in this verse reveal the agenda of the flesh in giving us a worldly identity?

7. Read Galatians 3:3. According to this verse, whose work is the flesh now trying to complete? Have you

ever thought about this "flavor" of religious or spiritual-looking flesh? What do you think is the answer to a struggle with this flavor of flesh?

8. Read Philippians 3:3–6. What do you think it means to "put confidence in the flesh"? What things were on Paul's fleshly résumé? What things might be on your own fleshly résumé (good looking or bad looking)? What would it look like for you to shift your confidence toward a new source of identity and purpose?

9. Read Genesis 4:7. How is sin described here? Is it a verb (action word) or a noun (thing) in this passage? Do you think recognizing sin in this way is important? If so, why?

10. Read Romans 7:17, 20. Read each of these verses slowly and carefully. What exactly does Paul say is happening when he ends up sinning? How might knowing this be helpful to us in a moment of temptation?

11. Read Romans 7:22–23 NASB. Where is this law (power) of sin located? What is it doing?

12. Read Romans 6:6–7, 11–12. Why were we crucified with Christ? What did it accomplish? When we're tempted, who do the "lusts" (or evil desires) really belong to now?

Part 7—Relax: You've Got Resurrection Life

1. Read Romans 5:12; Ephesians 2:1, 4–5; and Colossians 2:13. What is our core problem and what is God's solution?

2. Read Romans 7:10 and Galatians 3:21. What *two* things did the law fail to impart or bring?

3. Read John 10:10 and Romans 6:23. What was the main purpose of Jesus's ministry on earth and God's offer to us?

4. Read John 3:36 and 5:24. What decision can we make in order to benefit from God's offer to us? What is the result in our lives?

5. Read Romans 5:10. What causes us to be reconciled to God? What actually saves us? Had you ever thought about the difference between these two causes and effects?

6. Read John 11:25–26 and 14:6. How would you define eternal life using these verses? How does this help you see what life you possess?

7. Read John 14:19 and Hebrews 7:25; 13:5. *Why* do we live? *How long* will we live? And *what promise* does Jesus make to us? What effect does knowing this have on you personally?

8. Read Philippians 3:7–9. What is the most important thing in life to Paul? What specific benefits does he reap in having this focus? How does this passage speak to you as you go about setting life goals?

9. Read John 5:39–40 and 2 Peter 1:3. What good thing might distract us from the most important thing of all? How do we truly experience life and godliness?

10. Read 1 Corinthians 1:30–31 and 2 Corinthians 5:21. Exactly how holy are you? And exactly how righteous are you? How does the 2 Corinthians passage describe you?

11. Read Colossians 2:9–10. What does it mean to you personally to have been given *fullness* and *completeness* in Christ?

12. Read John 3:3–6 and 1 John 5:1. What does it mean to you personally that you are born of God's Spirit? What does this imply about your spiritual nature now?

13. Read Colossians 1:25–27. This passage describes a great mystery that was hidden for so long but has now been revealed. What is the mystery? Why is it such a big deal?

14. Read Galatians 2:20. Who are the two "I's" in this verse? What is the essential difference between how the first "I" lived and the second "I" now lives?

15. Read Philippians 1:21 and Colossians 2:6; 3:4. What does it mean to you that Christ is your life? What does "to live is Christ" mean to you in a practical sense?

Acknowledgments

First, I want to thank my wife, Katharine. Katharine, you are an amazing wife and an incredible mother to our son, Gavin. I love you with a love that comes from my very core, and as time goes by and I see more of who you are, I continue to be amazed at how blessed I am to have captured the attention of a woman with your character and beauty. Thank you for marrying me, and thank you for your constant support of my life and ministry.

To my son, Gavin, who is now seven years old, I want to say this: You have no idea, son, how much I love you and what I feel inside when I look at you and watch you play. It is indescribable. Our latest adventures at the ski resort with you so easily going down advanced slopes, right at my side, had me realizing that you have so quickly arrived at the friend stage. Gavin, I can already see who you are and who you are becoming, and I have a deep respect for your heart, your intelligence, and your creativity. I love you because you are my son, and I love you more than you can possibly imagine.

I want to thank my mother, Leslie Farley, for her many words of counsel and encouragement over the years. I was very fortunate to grow up in a home where the gospel was available to me on a regular basis. It was through my mother that I first became acquainted with the grace of God, and I am forever grateful to her for that.

A special thank-you goes to Andrea Heinecke and Alive Communications. I so appreciate all of your time and effort in helping me these last five years. And I want to thank Baker Books for partnering with me in this book ministry. In particular, I'd like to acknowledge Robert Hosack, Wendy Wetzel, Ruth Anderson, David Lewis, Erin Bartels, and Paula Gibson.

I am also very thankful for the leadership and members of Ecclesia for their consistent support. In particular, I want to thank Chip Polk, Rex Kennedy, Donny Bailey, Jordan Polk, and Kim Martin.

Finally, I want to thank you, the reader. If you enjoyed this book, consider passing it on to someone you care about.

Andrew Farley is the lead pastor of Church Without Religion. Visit www.churchwithoutreligion.com to select from hundreds of hours of free media and other resources.

Andrew is the bestselling author of *The Naked Gospel*, *God without Religion*, *Heaven Is Now*, and *The Art of Spiritual War*, and he is coauthor of *The Hurt & The Healer*, which he wrote with Bart Millard of MercyMe. Andrew's writings have been featured by national news outlets such as PBS, ABC, and FOX.

Andrew serves as president of Operation 220 (Operation220.org), a nonprofit Christian counseling ministry in Plano, Texas, and as president of Network 220 (Network220.org), an international association of more than one hundred Christ-centered counseling and training offices and churches.

Andrew lives with his wife, Katharine, and their son, Gavin, in West Texas, where Andrew works as a linguistics professor at Texas Tech University.

You can hear Andrew's live call-in radio program nationwide each Sunday on Sirius XM channel 131. In addition, you can connect with Andrew on Facebook (Facebook.com/DrAndrewFarley) and Twitter (@DrAndrewFarley) and find out more at www.andrewfarley.org.

The Naked Gospel

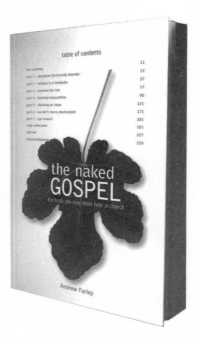

Jesus plus nothing. 100% natural. No additives.

The Naked Gospel is a chapter-by-chapter assault on the churchy jargon and double-talk of our day. It puts forth a message that is simple but life-changing. With a fresh take on Scripture and an unapologetic style, *The Naked Gospel* will challenge you to re-examine everything you thought you already knew.

Available now!

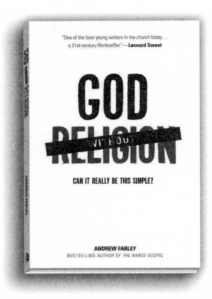

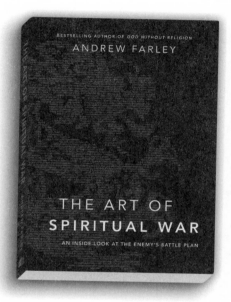